# BACK TO TAXACHUSETTS?

How the proposed tax amendment would
upend one of the nation's best economies.

By Greg Sullivan, Andrew Mikula & Liam Day

PIONEER INSTITUTE
PUBLIC POLICY RESEARCH

# ABOUT THE AUTHORS

**Gregory Sullivan** is Pioneer's Research Director. Prior to joining Pioneer, Sullivan served two five-year terms as Inspector General of the Commonwealth of Massachusetts and was a 17-year member of the Massachusetts House of Representatives. Greg is a Certified Fraud Investigator, and holds degrees from Harvard College, The Kennedy School of Public Administration, and the Sloan School at MIT.

**Andrew Mikula** is a former Economic Research Analyst at Pioneer Institute and current candidate for a Master's degree in Urban Planning at Harvard University.

**Liam Day** is a leader in the non-profit space in San Francisco and a writer. His experience in Boston includes serving as a youth worker and teacher, government service at the Boston Public Health Commission, including directing Child and Adolescent Health, and Director of Communications and Strategic Partnerships at Pioneer.

# ———— PRAISE FOR ————
# BACK TO TAXACHUSETTS?

"Massachusetts has finally established itself as a good place to do business. This has taken a lot of time and effort. It has also produced tremendous dividends for the Commonwealth. The notion of returning to Taxachusetts is simply wrongheaded and deleterious."

— William Achtmeyer, Acropolis Advisors

"Pioneer nailed it. This comprehensive study mirrors what I regularly faced while competing with other states for business development: *Taxes matter.* At 5%, Massachusetts is disadvantaged against some states but better than others. At 9%, forget about playing offense, we will be perpetually on defense as our golden egg-laying geese take flight to lower-cost harbors!"

— Jay Ash, Massachusetts Competitive Partnership and former State Economic Development Secretary

"The effects of tax policies and regulations on small businesses and business formation are well known. Pioneer's study effectively lays out the consequences of the constitutional tax amendment on entrepreneurs and should be heeded."

— John Friar, Executive Professor of Entrepreneurship and Innovation at the D'Amore-McKim School of Business, Northeastern University

"Pioneer Institute has done it again with *Back to Taxachusetts?* Their findings on the tax amendment proposal are a clear warning about what can go wrong when taxes are set by slogans and emotion, rather than research."

— Peter Forman, South Shore Chamber of Commerce

# PRAISE FOR
# BACK TO TAXACHUSETTS?

"Opinion leaders across the Commonwealth must read this book and understand the consequences of passing this massive tax hike. Without clear voter education, small business owners will be asking their legislators, associations and chambers of commerce 'where were you and why didn't you warn me?'"

— Jon B. Hurst, Retailers Association of Massachusetts

"This book reveals truths that proponents don't want you to know. The tax ensnares unintended people, even retirees. Promised higher spending on education and transportation disappear. Experiences from other states warn of big taxpayers leaving even faster. The more you tax an activity, the less of it you get. This economic rule may be hard for tax proponents to admit, but it's not too hard for voters to understand."

— Marc A. Miles, PhD, Former Assistant State Treasurer,
   State of New Jersey

"The data presented in *Back to Taxachusetts?* are compelling and frightening. The public must consider the negative effects of this surtax, and the numerous examples of how it backfired elsewhere before making the same mistake here in the Commonwealth."

— John Regan, Associated Industries of Massachusetts

"If you're somebody who cares about the future of our state, this book gives you all you need to make an informed decision on the graduated income tax proposal. As the authors show again and again, the tax will wreak havoc on the state's competitiveness and economic well-being."

— Brian Shortsleeve, Co-Founder, M33 Growth

# PIONEER INSTITUTE
## PUBLIC POLICY RESEARCH

Pioneer's **mission** is to develop and communicate dynamic ideas that advance prosperity and a vibrant civic life in Massachusetts and beyond.

Pioneer's **vision of success** is a state and nation where our people can prosper and our society thrive because we enjoy world-class options in education, healthcare, transportation, and economic opportunity, and where our government is limited, accountable, and transparent.

Pioneer **values** an America where our citizenry is well-educated and willing to test our beliefs based on facts and the free exchange of ideas, and committed to liberty, personal responsibility, and free enterprise.

# CONTENTS

# Foreword

If Pioneer Institute did not exist, it would be necessary to invent it. There is no other organization in the Commonwealth capable of producing the quantity and quality of analysis on pressing issues of public policy, such as income tax policy, that is found in this volume. Political discourse these days seems to turn more on tweets than position papers. But position papers remain crucial for informing our public debate, and we all owe a debt to Pioneer for its commitment to releasing sober, well-researched papers on such a breadth of subjects.

This particular volume addresses a proposal to amend the Massachusetts Constitution to impose a 4% surtax on all income over $1 million — an estimated $2 billion or more in new taxes each year — requiring the money raised to be spent on public education and transportation. Currently, our state Constitution mandates a flat tax, and the single income tax rate in Massachusetts is 5%.

Under the proposed constitutional amendment that rate would nearly double, to 9%, on any income over $1 million. Only a handful of states — California, Hawaii, Minnesota, New Jersey, and Oregon — have income tax brackets of 9% or higher.[1] With passage of the amendment, Massachusetts would jump near the front of the pack.

As explained by the analysis gathered in this volume, the proposed constitutional amendment poses significant risks that must be considered. As a matter of good governance, it is unwise to lock into the state Constitution both a particular tax rate and particular targets for increased spending (education and transportation). The Constitution is not easily amended; as seen with this proposal, it can take four years for a proposed amendment to go from introduction to the ballot.

What if, as Pioneer warns, the new tax causes high-net-worth individuals and important corporations to flee the state to lower-tax jurisdictions such as neighboring New Hampshire or sunny Florida, as happened when tax rates increased in Connecticut and New Jersey? What if some crisis (for example, a sudden global pandemic) suggests that the new revenues are better spent on priorities other than public education and transportation? The proposed amendment sets a dangerous precedent that will only be magnified if it succeeds and encourages special interests to sponsor additional proposals to lock state spending into specific categories.

As a matter of economic and social policy, the proposed amendment also is unwise. Pioneer has gathered substantial evidence demonstrating that increased state tax rates do, in fact, cause high-income individuals and corporations to relocate to more reasonable jurisdictions — states can kill the goose that lays the golden egg. In recent years, Massachusetts, which struggled so hard to shed the moniker of "Taxachusetts" that it bore in the 1980s, has been the beneficiary of that effect, taking in businesses that revolted against tax increases in neighboring Connecticut. It would be tragic if the Commonwealth reversed that inflow and began to lose businesses once again — a risk only increased, as Pioneer notes, by the ease of "working remotely" in so many industries, as revealed during the pandemic. As Pioneer also explains, the proposed amendment is punitive to many taxpayers whom no one would consider "rich," but who may have a sudden influx of income in one year as a result of selling a home or small business as they head into retirement.

Questions of tax policy and spending priorities are difficult. There are good reasons why legislatures, legislative staff, and public interest groups such as Pioneer spend so much time debating and analyzing the fine points of tax law and appropriations. These are not subjects that should be left to bumper sticker political campaigns, especially not when the results are then locked into the state Constitution. As Pioneer explains, the proposed amendment is not even honest with voters, suggesting to them that the new tax revenues must be spent on education and transportation, when the fungibility of money means that the legislature can spend the new revenue however it wants. If the Constitution is going to be amended, proponents should be transparent with voters about how the proposed amendment works.

Ultimately, voters will be asked in November 2022 to make a choice concerning the economic future of the Commonwealth. The ideas and analysis presented in this volume are crucial to informing that debate. I urge all those interested in preserving the Commonwealth's business climate to read Pioneer's work, and to forward it to friends and colleagues. Whichever way you decide to vote on the proposed amendment, make it an informed choice. Thank you to Pioneer for providing so much information in such a user-friendly volume.

### Kevin Martin

Kevin is a partner and co-chair of the Appellate Litigation group at Goodwin Procter LLP in Boston, Massachusetts, where he has practiced since 2001. He was counsel for the plaintiffs in Anderson v. Healey, the 2018 decision in which the Supreme Judicial Court excluded the graduated income tax from that year's ballot.

# Preface

For the past several years, Massachusetts union leaders and a majority of legislators have been working to promote a 4% surtax on the annual incomes of households and businesses that exceed $1 million. They seek to make this change in the Massachusetts state Constitution. It was first tried, literally, in 2018, when an initiative petition on the question was challenged before the Massachusetts Supreme Judicial Court. It was found unconstitutional.

The proposal re-emerged, like Lazarus if you are pro and more like a zombie if you are con, in 2019 as a petition of the legislature itself. The legislature was put before a constitutional convention in 2019, where it was approved, and then, in accordance with the legislative petition process, voted on at a second successive constitutional convention in June 2021. It was approved, interestingly, with the very same wording found unconstitutional by the Court in 2018. With the June 2021 approval, the proposal to amend the state constitution will appear on the statewide ballot in the fall of 2022.

The lead proponents of the amendment are the Massachusetts Teachers Association and the Service Employees International Union. A series of smaller advocacy and religious groups are following in their train. The promoters of the constitutional amendment refer to it as a "Fair Share Amendment," a wink and a nod to their frequent assertions that the measure would affect only the very wealthy, requiring them to pay what proponents define as their "fair share" of taxes.

After studying the topic at a level of depth that no other organization has, we fall squarely in the camp of the opponents. This brief volume is a distillation of two dozen academic studies that have examined the question from all angles.

As Kevin Martin suggests, there exists the structural issue of embedding both an exact rate and its intended purpose into the state constitution. There is wilful deception built into the wording of the amendment—the fiction that voting for the tax will force increased spending on education and transportation—a point that both sides sides explicitly agreed was not the case during the proceedings of Massachusetts' highest court in 2018.

Close analysis demonstrates that the people primarily impacted by the measure are businesses and retirees that are selling an asset, often a nest egg, at the end of a career. People and entities that are far from the imagined uber-wealthy who are trotted out by promoters of the new and permanent tax.

We further show that the surtax would endanger the long-term economic well-being of Massachusetts. Looking at decades of economic data, we demonstrate that the flight of businesses and wealth is already a prominent trend, especially to two low tax states: neighboring New Hampshire and sunny Florida. They assert that the new tax would prompt businesses and, yes, high-income residents to relocate to states with lower personal income tax rates, as well as the corollary: it would discourage them from moving to or establishing a presence in Massachusetts in the first place.

There is then the timing of the proposal. First, the push to amend Massachusetts' state constitution comes in the wake of 2017's federal tax overhaul, the Tax Cuts and Jobs Act, which includes a provision that caps the state and local tax (SALT) deductions taxpayers can take on their federal returns. The provision greatly magnifies the impact of the proposed tax increase.

While Congress may adopt changes to the deduction cap, as of this writing, the maximum state and local tax deduction is $10,000.

Second, the proposed amendment comes in the wake of the Covid pandemic, which has upended how we work—most likely on a permanent basis. Many knowledge-based businesses and really all jobs that do not require an in-person presence have become highly mobile. That makes the risk of business and wealth flight even greater among high-income residents and businesses alike.

Toward the end of this volume, we take stock of proponents' arguments in favor of the constitutional amendment, as well as the flawed studies they cite to bolster those viewpoints.

The purpose of this brief volume is, as Kevin Martin notes, ensuring that come November 2022, voters make an informed choice as to whether to embed a tax increase permanently in the state Constitution.

While aimed at a general audience, it is even more targeted at thought leaders, business leaders, media professionals — many of whom have heard that there is a tax issue up for a vote, but don't have a good understanding of what it means for them.

Of course, no one possesses a crystal ball. And that's why we turn to the empirical record — past trends and the experiences of other states — throughout this volume.

That is precisely where we begin. The first chapter looks at the experiences in Connecticut and California, both of which implemented higher taxes ostensibly focused on the wealthy.

These two states provide strong empirical evidence of the impact of tax policies similar to the proposed surtax amendment on job creation, home values, state spending, and so much more.

**James Stergios & Mary Connaughton**

Chapter 1

# Learning from Experiences in Other States

## Lessons from Connecticut

Long the wealthiest state in the country in terms of per capita income, Connecticut today is suffering from a corporate revolt that has seen mainstays like General Electric and Alexion Pharmaceuticals move valuable headquarters operations out of state. Less visible but still very real has been a steady outflow of wealth to other states, with high earners increasingly moving to low-tax states like Florida and North Carolina. Growth of the number of millionaires in the Constitution State is far below the national average.[2] Other economic indicators also point to trouble, including a stubbornly higher than average jobless rate. The state's billions of dollars of unfunded public employee pension obligations likewise illustrate the dire fiscal issues it faces.

There are a number of factors that contribute to the growing unease and turbulence in the Connecticut economy, generating headlines like *The Atlantic's* "What on Earth is Wrong with Connecticut?" and *Governing's* "The Fiscal Mess in America's Richest State." The Constitution State has lost 26,304 manufacturing jobs between 2008 and 2020, a drop of 14.1%, far greater than the U.S. drop of 5.3% over the same period.[3] Connecticut also ranked 49th among the states and D.C. in private sector wage gains and 48th in private sector employment gains between 2008 and 2020. It is one of only three states that never recovered to pre-Great Recession employment levels, alongside West Virginia and Wyoming. The state's once-vaunted regional casino gambling monopoly is also eroding amid new competition from Massachusetts, Rhode Island and New York.

Connecticut's embrace of an aggressive tax policy—including a sharp corporate tax rate increase—to pay for ballooning government expenditures has been a major contributor to the loss of bedrock employers. Higher corporate tax rates, combined with hikes in the personal income tax and, especially, the estate tax, also appear to be a factor driving away a growing number of the state's wealthiest residents.

## The Roots of Connecticut's Tax Crisis

Like the rest of the country, Connecticut has undergone dramatic changes during the past quarter century. These changes have led to losses of major businesses and, from the start of the Great Recession through January 2020, an actual decline in jobs. Insurance and financial services—pillars of the Connecticut economy—have taken hits as companies merge, consolidate, or move to what they perceive to be greener pastures.[4] In the past few years alone, Connecticut has lost General Electric and Alexion Pharmaceuticals to Massachusetts, and Aetna moved many of its top executives to New York.

In recent decades, Connecticut has seen chronic instability and turmoil when it comes to state government spending and taxes. The last 26 years have been punctuated by a cycle of budget showdowns in Hartford between various governors and legislative leaders. While the faces and names change, the results have typically been the same: sharp tax increases to cover the rising cost of a host of government services, with ballooning public employee pension obligations and health care costs leading the way.[5]

That's not the way it was supposed to work when Connecticut adopted the state's first income tax in 1991. Back in the 1980s, Connecticut had more in common with income tax-free New Hampshire, offering a lower-cost alternative to businesses and families than tax-and-spend states like New York and, at that time, Massachusetts.[6]

Until then, Connecticut had largely relied on a combination of a sales tax and corporate and capital gains levies to pay its bills, but revenue from all three plunged during the 1990–1991 recession, creating one of the worst state budget meltdowns in the country. When Gov. Lowell P. Weicker Jr., with help from Assembly and Senate Democrats, pushed through Connecticut's first income tax in 1991, one aim was to provide a more solid base for state finances. Critics warned the new tax would beget more spending, but Weicker and other supporters of the income tax argued that plans for a constitutional cap on spending would provide the necessary check.[7]

The spending cap has since fallen by the wayside as Connecticut lawmakers have voted to raise the income tax four times in the last 20 years, in 2003, 2009, 2011, and again in 2015. The top rate has shot up 77% since 1991, from 4.5% to 6.99%.[8] Behind the increases have been escalating public employee pension obligations and health benefits, as well as payments on Connecticut's large debt load, which has now reached into the tens of billions. From 1991 to 2016, these government expenditures increased by 174% above the rate of inflation.[9]

Connecticut's budget and tax woes have only intensified in the last few years, and former Gov. Dannel Malloy and state lawmakers increasingly targeted high earners and big companies to shoulder more of the burden. Faced with a $3.3 billion budget shortfall in 2011, the state turned to an array of tax hikes to help cover the gap. Along with raising the income tax, Gov. Malloy and state lawmakers doubled the surcharge tax for larger firms from 10 to 20%; rolled out a 7% luxury goods tax on yachts, jewelry, cars and clothes; and lowered the threshold for the estate tax from $3.5 million to $2 million.[10]

Gov. Malloy and lawmakers went back to the tax well in 2015 when they faced yet another massive budget deficit, again tapping the state's major corporations and the wealthy to close the gap. That year's budget hiked the top rate for individuals making over $250,000 and couples more than $500,000 from 6.7 to 6.9%, rising to 6.99% for single filers earning more than $500,000 and couples pulling down more than $1 million. Connecticut resident trusts and estates saw their taxes jump to 6.99 % as well.[11] There was also an increase in the relatively new luxury goods tax—covering everything from cars worth more than $50,000 to clothing valued at over $1,000 —from 7% to 7.75%.[12]

Corporations didn't get off any easier. The 10% corporate tax surcharge was extended through 2021, while companies were prohibited from reducing their taxes by more than 50% through the use of tax credits, down from the previous 70%. In recent years, Connecticut has also expanded its pass-through entity tax base, effectively raised taxes on pass-through entity owners, and reduced tax credits for pass-through entities.[13] A decision to move towards a unitary reporting system in which major companies would have to pay taxes on operations beyond Connecticut's borders drew stern warnings from GE and Aetna, among other companies.[14]

The upshot is that, after years of increases, Connecticut's state and local tax burden topped 12.6% by 2012, second in the country only to New York and up from a low of 9.9% in 1980.[15] By 2020, Connecticut had one of the latest "Tax Freedom" days in the nation on April 25, three weeks later than Florida and nine days later than the country as a whole.[16] The state's escalating array of tax hikes has not gone unnoticed by those at the top end of the income ladder.

According to Tax Foundation rankings published in 2016, Connecticut ranked highest in total state/local tax burden per capita nationwide and ranked second in state-local tax burden as a percent of state income (see Figure 1) based on an analysis of fiscal year 2012 data. Massachusetts, by comparison, ranked 6th and 12th, respectively.[17]

While a budget showdown in Hartford again grabbed headlines in 2017, proposals for yet another income tax hike and for a levy on hedge funds went nowhere amid increasing push back by the business community. In October 2019, revenue projections still showed that the status quo would produce billion-dollar budget deficits by fiscal year 2022, despite the steps the state took to increase revenue by more than $2.5 billion in the 2019 legislative session.[18] During the COVID-19 pandemic, Connecticut has relied largely on its Rainy Day Fund to balance its budget, an unsustainable strategy that does nothing to mitigate a billion-dollar rise in fixed costs.[19] Left to foot the bill for Connecticut's fiscal meltdown on multiple fronts, major employers and some of its wealthiest families and individuals have been heading for the exits.

# Figure 1. List of states by state & local tax burden, 2020[20]

| Inc per cap | State | State & local tax burden as a share of state income | Rank | State & local tax burden per capita | Rank |
|---|---|---|---|---|---|
| 65644 | New York | 13.8% | 1 | $9,059 | 1 |
| 72213 | Connecticut | 10.6% | 10 | $7,655 | 2 |
| 64924 | New Jersey | 10.7% | 7 | $6,947 | 3 |
| 52669 | North Dakota | 12.7% | 2 | $6,689 | 4 |
| 53145 | Hawaii | 12.5% | 3 | $6,643 | 5 |
| 68233 | Massachusetts | 9.6% | 25 | $6,550 | 6 |
| 60512 | Maryland | 10.4% | 13 | $6,293 | 7 |
| 60156 | California | 10.3% | 14 | $6,196 | 8 |
| 54919 | Minnesota | 11.2% | 6 | $6,151 | 9 |
| 51976 | Vermont | 11.6% | 4 | $6,029 | 10 |
| 53943 | Illinois | 10.7% | 8 | $5,772 | 11 |
| 52379 | Rhode Island | 10.6% | 9 | $5,552 | 12 |
| 58550 | Washington | 9.1% | 30 | $5,328 | 13 |
| 46570 | Maine | 11.4% | 5 | $5,309 | 14 |
| 53144 | Pennsylvania | 9.7% | 22 | $5,155 | 15 |
| 50663 | Nebraska | 10.1% | 17 | $5,117 | 16 |
| 47458 | Iowa | 10.5% | 11 | $4,983 | 17 |
| 58397 | New Hampshire | 8.4% | 41 | $4,905 | 18 |
| 50350 | Delaware | 9.7% | 23 | $4,884 | 19 |
| 49290 | Wisconsin | 9.9% | 19 | $4,880 | 20 |
| 55335 | Colorado | 8.8% | 33 | $4,869 | 21 |
| 55306 | Virginia | 8.7% | 36 | $4,812 | 22 |
| 48372 | Oregon | 9.8% | 21 | $4,740 | 23 |
| 56377 | Wyoming | 8.3% | 44 | $4,679 | 24 |
| 46651 | Ohio | 10.0% | 18 | $4,665 | 25 |
| 48869 | Kansas | 9.5% | 27 | $4,643 | 26 |
| 46914 | Nevada | 9.6% | 26 | $4,504 | 27 |
| 43938 | Louisiana | 9.9% | 20 | $4,350 | 28 |
| 49554 | South Dakota | 8.6% | 38 | $4,262 | 29 |
| 46258 | Michigan | 9.1% | 31 | $4,209 | 30 |
| 47929 | Texas | 8.7% | 35 | $4,170 | 31 |
| 39521 | New Mexico | 10.4% | 12 | $4,110 | 32 |

| | | | | | |
|---|---|---|---|---|---|
| 56794 | Alaska | 7.2% | 50 | $4,089 | 33 |
| 44002 | Utah | 9.2% | 29 | $4,048 | 34 |
| 41520 | Arkansas | 9.6% | 24 | $3,986 | 35 |
| 44180 | North Carolina | 9.0% | 32 | $3,976 | 36 |
| 38644 | West Virginia | 10.2% | 15 | $3,942 | 37 |
| 45312 | Montana | 8.6% | 39 | $3,897 | 38 |
| 40999 | Kentucky | 9.5% | 28 | $3,895 | 39 |
| 45225 | Indiana | 8.6% | 37 | $3,889 | 40 |
| 45744 | Missouri | 8.4% | 43 | $3,842 | 41 |
| 44536 | Georgia | 8.4% | 40 | $3,741 | 42 |
| 42094 | Idaho | 8.8% | 34 | $3,704 | 43 |
| 36375 | Mississippi | 10.1% | 16 | $3,674 | 44 |
| 47869 | Florida | 7.6% | 48 | $3,638 | 45 |
| 42081 | South Carolina | 8.4% | 42 | $3,535 | 46 |
| 43634 | Oklahoma | 8.1% | 47 | $3,534 | 47 |
| 42505 | Arizona | 8.2% | 46 | $3,485 | 48 |
| 44950 | Tennessee | 7.6% | 49 | $3,416 | 49 |
| 40467 | Alabama | 8.3% | 45 | $3,359 | 50 |

## Stagnant Economy

Like many states in the Northeast, Connecticut has been adversely impacted by some significant long-term economic trends. The Constitution State has seen a steady drop in manufacturing jobs amid growth in lower-paid sectors like health, education, and tourism. Moreover, Connecticut residents face some of the highest housing costs in the country.

Connecticut's economy has dramatically underperformed the nation and New England over the past decade, a period of near constant state budget emergencies in Hartford, almost inevitably followed by sharp tax increases. It is part of a larger trend, with Connecticut's recovery from the Great Recession markedly slower than the country as a whole and slower than its more economically dynamic neighbor to the north, Massachusetts.

## Figure 2. Non-farm employment growth rate by state, January 2008 – January 2020[21]

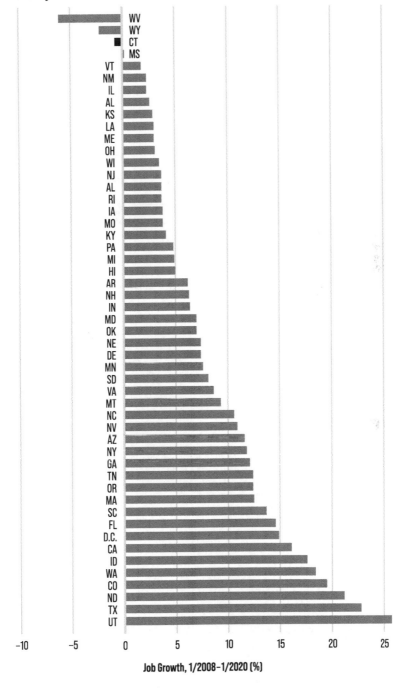

Job Growth, 1/2008–1/2020 (%)

Between the pre-Great Recession employment peak of January 2008 and January 2020, just before the pandemic hit, only three states failed to restore employment to pre-recession levels: Connecticut, West Virginia, and Wyoming. Unlike the post-recession struggles of West Virginia and Wyoming, however, Connecticut's stagnant economy is harder to link to a heavy reliance on energy production and natural resource extraction. Connecticut had 11,800 fewer seasonally-adjusted jobs in January 2020 than in January 2008 (see Figure 2).

**Figure 3. Cumulative nonfarm employment gains in the U.S. and Connecticut, January 2008 – January 2020[22]**

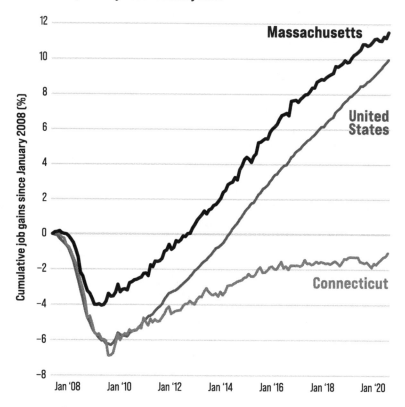

A July 2017 report from Connecticut state comptroller Kevin Lembo predicted the state would recover its jobs lost during the Great Recession in "a little over two years."[23] Instead, Connecticut's recovery stalled, and after Lembo's report was published, the state continued to lose jobs on net through the summer of 2019. To put this in a national perspective, U.S. employment had surpassed pre-Great Recession levels by May 2014. Figure 3 compares recession job recovery in Connecticut to the U.S. as a whole, showing that in January 2020 the U.S. had 10% more seasonally-adjusted nonfarm jobs than it did in January 2008, while Connecticut had 1% fewer jobs.[24]

**Figure 4. Private Sector Job Growth by NAICS Sector in the United States and Connecticut, 2008–2020**[25]

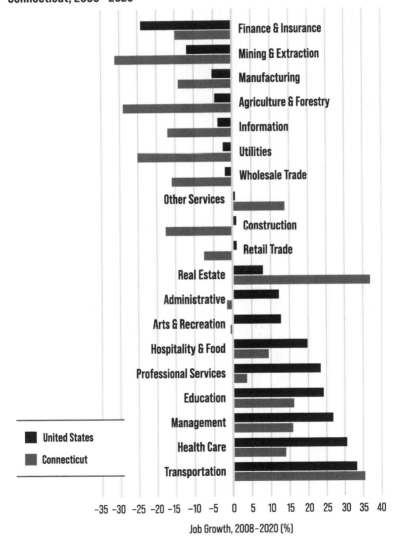

## Figure 5. Private sector wage growth by state, 2008 – 2020[26]

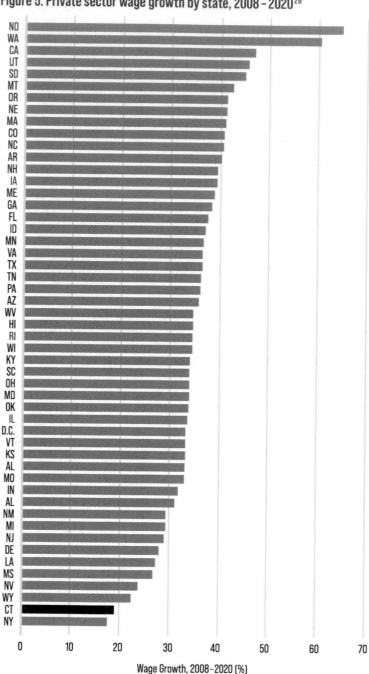

Wage Growth, 2008-2020 (%)

It's difficult to pin this economic stagnation on any one industry. Between 2008 and 2020, Connecticut underperformed the U.S. in 14 of the 18 private industry sectors classified by the North American Industry Classification System (NAICS). Connecticut suffered double-digit job losses in eight of those sectors, including financial services (−14.9%), manufacturing (−14.%), construction (−17.6%), and utilities (−25.1%), among others (see Figure 4).

Another useful measure of the dissonance between Connecticut and the rest of the country in terms of economic performance is private sector compensation growth. Connecticut ranked 49th among the states in private sector wage gains from 2008 to 2020, with private sector paychecks increasing just 19.1% in the Constitution State compared to 34.2% in the U.S. as a whole (see Figure 5).[27] By comparison, private sector paychecks in Massachusetts increased 41.0% during the same period, beating the national average. Connecticut also underperformed the U.S. in wage growth in 14 of the 18 NAICS sectors.

Among the reasons for the slow private sector wage growth in Connecticut post-Great Recession is that, even as the state failed to add back, on par with other states, the jobs it had lost, the new jobs that were being created were not as high-paying as the ones it had been losing. A 2016 report by the Connecticut Commission for Economic Competitiveness found that jobs added by the state's new growth industries—health care, food service, and education—had an average annual pay of $54,018. More remunerative fields, like IT, manufacturing, and construction, where wages average $75,246, were shedding jobs.[28]

According to the State Economic Competitiveness Index series published by the American Legislative Exchange Council (ALEC), Connecticut's economic outlook ranked 32nd among the states in 2009 (with 1 being best and 50 worst).[29] By 2020, it had slipped to 40th. In a more recent report, ALEC described Connecticut's sluggish GDP growth and persistent domestic out-migration as especially alarming.[30] It also ranked Connecticut as the single worst state in terms of economic performance between 2008 and 2018. The same report found that a 2019 tax increase threatened to decrease Connecticut's economic outlook rank from 40th to 44th.[31]

## Figure 6. Private Sector Wage Growth by NAICS Sector in the United States and Connecticut, 2008 – 2020[32]

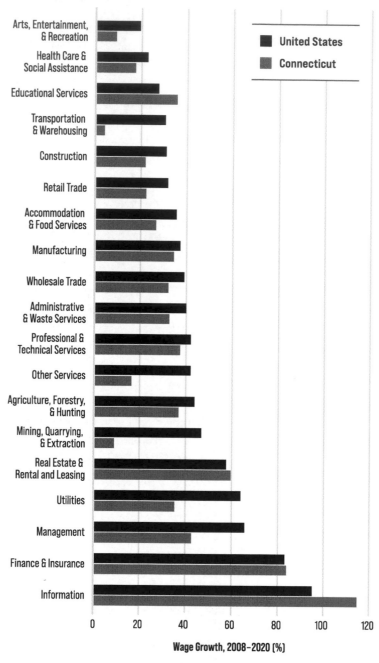

Wage Growth, 2008–2020 [%]

Repeated budget crises and tax hikes don't just result in a sluggish economy and job losses. Homeowners are also taking a hit. Connecticut ranked dead last among the 50 states and Washington, D.C. in house price appreciation between 2012 and 2020 (see Figure 7).[33] In Fairfield County, which is well-known for its high concentration of wealthy individuals and large corporations, home values remained 18% below their 2006 peak as of 2019.[34]

The economic damage done by Connecticut's perennial budget deficits has apparently been compounded by the state's decision to deal with them by repeatedly hiking taxes, according to economist Nicholas Perna. "Deficits are not just corrosive to confidence in the business climate, but eliminating them through taxes or spending cuts is a drag on the economy," Perna noted in an interview with the CT Mirror.[35]

Looking ahead, Connecticut's outlook is clouded by high taxes and high debt. The state has the 6th highest property taxes and 12th highest personal income taxes in the country.[36] It is one of just 11 states to have its own estate tax, and Connecticut's base estate tax rate of 10% is tied for second highest in the nation.[37] The state's budget for fiscal years 2020 and 2021 included hundreds of millions of dollars of tax hikes and revenue grabs, all while burdening the business community with minimum wage increases and paid family and medical leave obligations. The General Assembly also called for an exploratory study of a payroll tax on employers, which was later implemented in January 2021.[38] Meanwhile, consumers have to contend with an additional 1% tax on restaurant meals and expansions of the state sales tax to cover motor vehicle parking, dry cleaning, interior design services, and other activities.[39]

## Corporate Exodus

Faced with a sluggish economy and constant turmoil over the state budget and taxes, some of Connecticut's top companies have and continue to move to other states. This corporate exodus threatens to further exacerbate the state's already serious tax and budget woes.

General Electric was among the most visible of the companies that left Connecticut. In 2016, the company decided to move its headquarters to South Boston's booming waterfront with a promise to employ up to 800 people there, including many highly paid executives, though recent estimates pin the number at closer to 250.[40]

Despite this disappointing result for Massachusetts, there isn't much of a silver lining for Connecticut, which simply failed to maintain the friendly business climate and political favoritism that GE had come to expect.[41] While the tax incentives used to lure GE to Boston rightfully remain controversial, by 2016 Massachusetts was clearly in a better position than Connecticut to pour money into corporate tax breaks after gross public debt had fallen for five straight years as a percentage of GDP. By contrast, gross public debt rose in Connecticut as a share of GDP every year from 2007 to 2020.[42]

GE's exit has only made the state's debt crisis worse. General Electric once paid roughly $1.9 million a year to the Town of Fairfield alone, and hundreds of well-paid GE executives no longer pay Connecticut income taxes after the company's move to Boston.[43]

Still, perhaps the biggest damage resulting from GE's exit is to Connecticut's once solid reputation as a good place to do business. Connecticut's failure to hang onto the crown jewel of its corporate community—or at least to make a reasonable show of responding to GE's concerns—has helped make the Constitution State a poster child for states seemingly hostile or indifferent to the concerns of business, sparking negative business press coverage.

GE's move has paved the way for defections by other companies, such as Alexion Pharmaceuticals, which announced plans to move to Boston by mid-2018, despite having to pay back a $20 million loan from the State of Connecticut and a $6 million grant.[44] The company is now located just a 10-minute walk from GE's South Boston headquarters. Aetna also seemed unhappy about the direction of Connecticut's tax and budget policies, threatening to move its headquarters to New York.[45] Aetna even offered Connecticut lawmakers a warning, tying the issue of whether it will keep a substantial number of employees in Connecticut over the long term to the state's economic health and the ability of political leaders to put state finances on a "sound financial footing."[46] While Aetna's headquarters remain in Connecticut as of 2021, its public outcry over state taxation was particularly unsettling given the company's roots in Connecticut that go back to 1853.[47]

It would be hard to argue that no one saw this corporate rebellion brewing. GE and Aetna were out front in warning Connecticut's political establishment about the potential consequences of its seemingly endless cycle of budget crises and subsequent tax hikes. With a $700 million tax hike in the works, Aetna, Travelers and GE all released statements on the same day in June 2015 warning Governor Malloy and legislators of the potential consequences of moving forward. GE warned it would "seriously consider whether it makes any sense to remain in Connecticut," while Aetna made clear "such an action will result in Aetna looking to reconsider the viability of continuing major operations in the state."[48]

Connecticut lawmakers passed the tax package anyway. One senator claimed that the increases, which supporters argued would be used to pay for overhauls to the state's transportation system, signaled "a brighter day" ahead.[49]

The plan included a "unitary tax" requiring companies to pay taxes on their subsidiaries and operations in other jurisdictions, not just Connecticut. With its global footprint, GE had been particularly vocal in its concerns about that part of the package.[50]

## Voting With Their Feet

It is not just Connecticut's leading corporations that are reconsidering whether to stay in the Constitution State. Some of the state's wealthiest families and individuals have also been voting with their feet.

Most individuals don't have a company's megaphone through which to broadcast their displeasure over state budget and tax policy. For myriad reasons, high-net-worth individuals may also be loath to take actions that draw attention to their status or to inject themselves into volatile and contentious public debates.

## Figure 7. Home value appreciation by state, Q1 2012 to Q1 2020[51]

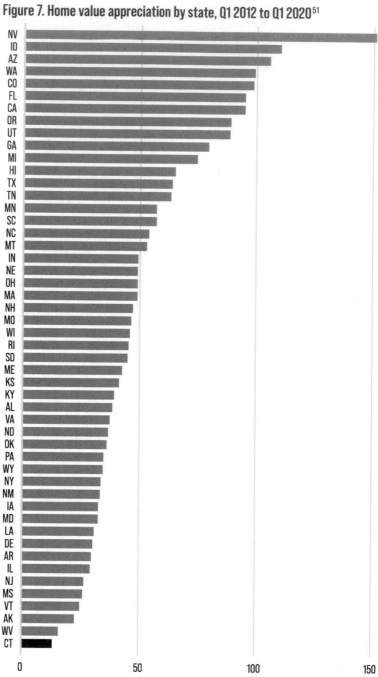

Home appreciation, 1/2012-1/2020 [%]

However, in 2012 (tax year 2011), the IRS began to track "Gross-Migration File" data, which includes changes in address reported on income tax returns. The data track both "inflows"— taxpayers moving into a particular state or county—and "outflows," or those leaving. The returns are also grouped by age and adjusted gross income (AGI) in tiers ranging from $0–$10,000 to $200,000 and up. The data afford researchers the opportunity to study the inward and outward state migration of individuals with relatively high incomes.

There are critics of this type of analysis who note that just because someone moves out of state doesn't mean the job and taxable income they are leaving behind are lost, arguing that someone else will be hired to fill the position.

Critics have also taken aim at studies arguing that state tax rates are the primary reason why some states are losing population, especially among wealthier residents. There are obviously many factors driving migration from some states and towards others, including a preference for the sunnier climes of Florida and Texas by retirees from the chillier Northeast. Housing costs and economic factors are also important, especially if opportunities for advancement and profit are more abundant elsewhere.

Yet it would be disingenuous to say that tax rates and additional levies like estate and inheritance taxes play no role in why some states are losing population to others that don't have income or estate taxes. That is especially true in the case of Connecticut, which has lost a significant number of its wealthiest citizens during a time of rising tax rates amid lackluster economic performance.

In 2018 alone, Connecticut lost more than $1.2 billion in net AGI migration.[52] On a per capita basis, only Washington D.C., New York, Illinois, Alaska, and New Jersey lost more.[53] Over the period 2012–2018, net AGI losses from interstate movement totaled $12.3 billion in the Constitution state, more than Massachusetts' corresponding figure of $8.5 billion, despite the fact that Connecticut has about half of Massachusetts' population.

Overall, residents filing 27,537 tax returns with an AGI of at least $200,000 (hereafter, "high-income taxpayers") moved out of Connecticut between 2012 and 2018, far outpacing the 20,174 tax returns filed by those who moved in. Tellingly, the average annual income of the high-income taxpayers who moved out, $765,958, well exceeds the average income of those who moved in, $634,364. While migration created a decline in AGI in every income bracket tracked by the IRS from 2012 to 2018, top earners made up over two-thirds of Connecticut's tax revenue migration losses during the period, a product of their disproportionate wealth and high out-migration rates (see Figure 8).

On a per-capita basis, Connecticut's net migration of AGI among high-income taxpayers was second worst in the country from 2012 to 2018, with only Washington, D.C. seeing more taxable income flee.[54] Over this period, Connecticut received an average of 121,749 tax returns per year from taxpayers with an AGI of $200,000 or more. Its net AGI out-migration of taxpayers in this income category was a staggering $8.29 billion, representing an average AGI loss of $765,958 for every high-income taxpayer who left. While Connecticut and D.C. were losing net AGI due to out-migration of high-income taxpayers, many states, led by Florida, had net positive gains in AGI among high-income taxpayers (see Figure 9). In just seven years, 122,341 high-income taxpayers moved to Florida, adding $3,244 of taxable income on net to Florida's AGI for each resident the state had in 2012, a total of $62.6 billion.[55]

The decision by some of the state's wealthiest families to move elsewhere has contributed to a decline in tax revenue that has only deepened Connecticut's latest budget crisis. And state officials have announced public recognition of this issue. Taxes paid by the state's top 100 taxpayers plunged by 45% from 2015 to 2016 alone, adding up to a $200 million hit.[56] Despite this decrease in wealthy taxpayers, in 2016 the richest 3% of Connecticut households were still responsible for 41% of income tax payments.[57]

In 2010, there were 11 Connecticut billionaires on the Forbes 400 list of the wealthiest Americans.[58] By 2020, that list had shrunk to five.[59] Of the previous decade's 11, four had moved to Florida and one had died.[60] Meanwhile, two had fallen off of the list for financial reasons and another, logistics entrepreneur

Bradley Jacobs, had joined the list for the first time. The four who fled to Florida, including Paul Tudor Jones, Edward Lampert, Thomas Peterffy, and C. Dean Metropoulos, had a combined net worth of $34.1 billion as of November 2021. While calculating how much each would have paid in taxes is difficult, as many of the details of each individual's investment income and salaries are not public, the stock market often nets them tens of millions of dollars every day, implying a nine-figure loss of revenue for the State of Connecticut.[61]

**Figure 8. Net AGI loss due to migration in Connecticut by income group, 2012–2018**

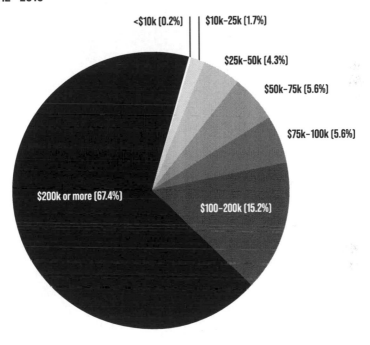

## Figure 9. Per capita net AGI loss due to migration of high-income taxpayers by state, 2012–2018

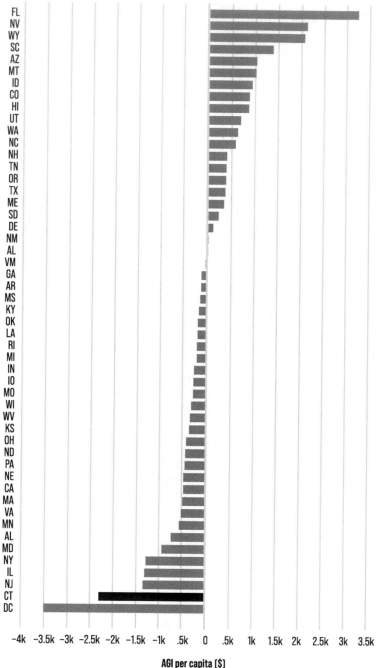

AGI per capita ($)

Beyond out-migration of high-income residents, a number of additional factors may be fueling the drop in taxes paid by Connecticut's wealthiest residents. State revenue officials point to a decline in the hedge fund industry, for example.[62] And while migration rates of the wealthy are often relatively low, Kevin B. Sullivan, commissioner of the Connecticut Department of Revenue Services, admitted in 2016 that "five or six of the highest earners could have a measurable impact on the revenue stream." The state's over-reliance on the wealthy to fill state coffers has even led it to track how much some of its most affluent individuals should be paying in taxes each quarter.[63]

Moreover, Connecticut's wealthiest families may be taking other measures short of completely relocating to protect their income as the state repeatedly raises rates. Stories abound of multi-millionaires who have changed their tax domiciles to Florida, despite continuing to operate businesses in Connecticut or New York City.[64] After a brief lag, it seems that efforts to evade taxation have caught up with tax hikes. The amount of taxes paid by the top 100 jumped after rates climbed in 2011 and 2015, only to fall again the following years, state revenue officials have said.[65]

It's not just about the income tax, either. The wealthiest taxpayers also pay close attention to estate and gift taxes, which can fall heavily on those in the highest tax brackets. Connecticut is one of a dwindling number of jurisdictions with an estate tax and the only state with a gift tax.

Twelve states still had an estate tax in 2020, down from 15 in 2015 after Tennessee, Delaware, and New Jersey all abolished the levy.[66] Several other states have decided to raise their thresholds for applying the tax, with New York notably upping it to $5.25 million.[67]

But under pressure to meet the rising cost of ever-growing public employee pension obligations, Connecticut has moved in the opposite direction. During the 2011 budget crisis, the state lowered the threshold for its estate tax, which tops out at 12%, from $3.5 million to $2 million.[68] Four years later, amid another budget showdown, state lawmakers lifted a $12,500 cap on probate fees, while estates over $2 million had court fees raised to 0.5%, enough so probate costs topped $1 million for some large estates.[69]

While Connecticut is currently set to raise its estate tax threshold to the federal level of $11.6 million by 2023, the economic damage from its era of recklessness has already been done.[70]

Alongside its income tax hike, Connecticut's decision to double down on the estate tax has arguably been a significant factor contributing to the outflow of wealthy families and their assets since 2013. A 2008 study by Connecticut revenue and budget officials zeroed in on the reasons why residents and retirees were leaving the state. More than half the estate planners surveyed for the study reported having clients who changed their main residence from Connecticut or moved to another state altogether "primarily" due to the estate tax.[71]

The study found that the average estate of those who left Connecticut was $7.5 million, which would have equated to $705,200 in potential estate taxes, while their average taxable income was $446,000. This resulted in a loss to the Connecticut treasury of nearly $22,000 in income taxes from each family who left.[72] The top four destinations were Florida, New Hampshire, Arizona and North Carolina, none of which have estate taxes. The top four reasons clients gave for moving out of Connecticut were the state's income tax, its estate tax, the New England climate, and already spending part of the year out of state.[73]

The study by Connecticut revenue officials also noted it's not that hard to change your principal address for tax purposes given the options opened up by modern travel and the personal computer and internet. It can be as simple as listing a second home as a main residence.

The ease with which Connecticut's highest earners are able to side-step estate taxes and the state's 12% gift tax, another levy unpopular with the wealthy, were highlighted in an op-ed by David DeLucia, a retired executive living in Darien after a long and successful career on Wall Street.[74] DeLucia notes that all but one of his "super wealthy" friends in Connecticut have since moved to Florida. He is particularly irked by Connecticut's gift tax, noting it is the only state with such a fee. After a lifetime of paying taxes, DeLucia feels he has paid his fair share and then some. "Wealthy people have options, especially mobility," DeLucia writes. "If I sell my Connecticut home, move to any other state and then make gifts of my wealth to my heirs, I save them millions of dollars. My super wealthy friends call this the 'free move.' You can move out of Connecticut and the gift tax savings more than offsets the cost of the move and the new home purchase. Why wouldn't anyone do this?"

When the wealthy leave, the state doesn't just lose the income taxes they would have paid. Their spending on "expensive cars, big homes, expensive jewelry... fancy restaurants" also moves with them, not to mention wages paid to "landscapers, plumbers, electricians, etc.," DeLucia argues. "Connecticut politicians seem wedded to their simple strategy of, "Let's keep raising taxes on the remaining corporations and the wealthy so they can all pay their fair share," DeLucia writes. "This one-trick pony only works for so long and, I might add, when you put on too much weight, even a strong pony collapses."

Out-migration of the wealthy is part of a national trend that is seeing the wealthy move out of New York, New Jersey and other states to escape estate taxes. Nor is it necessarily required that the affluent actually move anywhere to avoid estate taxes. In some cases, the highest earners aren't going anywhere, just moving assets into trusts in states without estate taxes like Delaware and Alaska. William Lipkind, a New Jersey lawyer, told Bloomberg News he routinely moves clients' assets out of state to avoid estate taxes, with the amount ranging from several hundred thousand dollars to hundreds of millions. "I can't sit with a client who has a substantial portfolio or is contemplating selling his business without putting the strategy on the table," Lipkind said. "You scratch your head and say, 'Why pay if we don't have to?'"[75]

As a result, Connecticut's high estate tax rate hasn't translated to higher revenues. In 2009, estate and gift taxes made up 1.9% of total tax revenues, declining to 1.1% by 2019.[76] This may also be a sign that would-be taxpayers have found ways of avoiding them.

## No Longer Taxachusetts

Defenders of Connecticut's tax policies point to the fact that it has lost a considerable amount of wealth over the last few years to Massachusetts. Given the Commonwealth's old Taxachusetts label, they claim this demonstrates that Connecticut's tax policies are not a major factor in the exodus of wealthy taxpayers from the state.

But this argument is rooted in an outdated view of the Bay State's tax and budget policies. Connecticut has hiked its income tax four times since 2003; Massachusetts has hiked its income tax just once in the last 25 years.

In the midst of a dire budget crisis during the 1990–1991 recession, Massachusetts lawmakers voted to hike the income tax to 6.25% and then drop it down again in 1992 to 5.95%.[77] Nearly a decade later, Massachusetts approved a ballot question to bring the income tax rate back down to 5%. State lawmakers later attached a series of conditions designed to make the decline in the income tax rate a gradual process, with a .05% drop each year in which certain revenue markers were met. By 2020, the rate had reached its target of 5.0%.[78]

State lawmakers roundly rejected a proposal by Gov. Deval Patrick in 2013 to hike the income tax rate back to 6.25% to spend more on transportation and infrastructure projects.[79] While Massachusetts adopted a combined tax reporting system of the type GE protested so vehemently in Connecticut, it also knocked its corporate tax rate down from 9.5% to 8%.[80]

Overall, from 1977 to 2012, Massachusetts saw one of the largest tax reductions in the country, with residents' local and state tax burden dropping from 12.3% to 10.3%. Only Alaska and North and South Dakota saw bigger drops.[81] Once one of the worst performers, Massachusetts is now solidly in the middle ranks of the Tax Foundation's Business Tax Climate Index.[82]

The Bay State's relative restraint on taxes and spending helped set the stage for a quarter century of strong growth following the state budget battles and crises of 1988–1991. Massachusetts has created more and better jobs than Connecticut and other states across the Northeast, and real per capita income more than tripled from 1980 to 2019.[83]

Overall, Massachusetts gained some 411,000 net jobs from 2008 to 2020 for an increase of 12.5%, according to Pioneer Institute research. The state recovered all the jobs lost during the Great Recession and then some, with more than 3.7 million people working in Massachusetts in 2020, compared to 3.3 million in 2008.[84] Before the COVID-19 pandemic, the state unemployment rate hovered near 3%, a 20-year low and down from 8.8% at the height of the Great Recession.[85]

The Bay State's lower taxes and more vibrant economy are attracting or creating millionaires at nearly twice the rate of Connecticut. Massachusetts saw the number of millionaires increase by 84.5% from 2009 to 2019, making it and New Hampshire the only northeastern states in the top one-third of the list of the 50 states and Washington D.C..[86] That's also well above Connecticut's 57.3% millionaire growth rate.

Connecticut has turned repeatedly to its wealthiest taxpayers to cover spending increases and is now suffering the consequences. Connecticut's governor and top legislative leaders were equally optimistic before the state's last major tax hike in 2015. Mark Bergman, a spokesman for Gov. Malloy, called it a "historic investment" financed by tapping the state's richest families and companies, adding that "we are asking our wealthiest and our corporate community to help pay for a transformational transportation and infrastructure system that will benefit Connecticut's economy for decades to come."[87]

Connecticut's legislature and governor shrugged off warnings from major employers like GE and Aetna that they would consider moving out of state if potentially damaging provisions like a unitary tax reporting system were passed. Years of red flags and other signs that the Constitution State's wealthiest families were just as unhappy with the state's tax policies also went unheeded.

Consequently, the state's third tax increase in six years failed to usher in a new era of prosperity or even solve Connecticut's persistent budget woes. Instead, Connecticut's economic growth practically ground to a halt in 2016, with a drop in income tax revenue from the state's wealthiest taxpayers triggering another budget crisis in 2017.

This time, legislative leaders rejected plans to boost the state income tax for couples making more than $1 million annually to 7.49%.[88] Malloy, who just two years before had led the charge for higher taxes on corporations and the wealthy, talked lawmakers down from plans to impose a special tax on hedge funds, siding with Republicans who argued it would drive millionaires from the state.[89]

While the Massachusetts economy has proven far more resilient and dynamic in recent years, there's no reason to think a similar scenario couldn't repeat itself here. Like Connecticut, the Commonwealth is reliant on a relatively small number of wealthy taxpayers, who foot a sizable chunk of the state's bills.[90]

There are many reasons why wealthy families and corporations opt to leave one state for another, from weather to the business climate. While taxes are not the sole factor, they are nevertheless a consideration for companies and wealthy families alike, who routinely draw upon sophisticated advice from financial planners, accountants, and tax lawyers. Moreover, taxes are a factor that can become more important as rates escalate.

For those with the means to relocate, mobility has never been easier. The rise of instant communications and the ability to do business anywhere and anytime make it fairly easy to change one's permanent address and effectively move income to a state with lower income taxes, or none at all.

Connecticut provides a sobering real-world example of how a seemingly attractive tax-the-rich scheme can backfire badly on a state, turning rosy projections of revenue gains to real-life losses, and damaging business confidence in the process.

We next turn our attention to another state that offers lessons to Massachusetts on the consequences of progressive taxation: California.

## A 2012 Tax Hike Cost California Billions of Dollars in Economic Activity

In the aftermath of the Great Recession of 2007–2009, the State of California faced a series of difficult budget decisions. In state lawmakers' own words, these decisions resulted in some $56 billion in cuts to "education, police and fire protection, healthcare, and other critical state and local services."[91] Then, in 2012, the same lawmakers reached a dubious conclusion, namely that "raising new tax revenue is an investment in our future that will put California back on track for growth and success."[92] This is the context in which the legislature, and later the state's voters, passed Proposition 30, a momentous tax hike that, among other things, raised the state's highest marginal income tax rate by three percentage points.

Often packaged as a temporary move necessary to avoid $6 billion in additional core service cuts, Proposition 30 has likely stifled business activity in the state, especially among pass-through entities.[93] The elevated income tax rates were later extended beyond their initial 2018 expiration date to 2030, perhaps cementing in place the legislation's detrimental economic effects for decades to come.[94]

### The Wealthy Take Flight

Research into the impact of California's Proposition 30 on migration was scarce for the first several years after its passage.[95] This was largely due to an absence of administrative "microdata" that would adequately allow researchers to isolate the effect of Proposition 30 from broader macroeconomic trends and changes in the federal tax code. That changed in October 2019, when two NBER economists, Joshua Rauh and Ryan Shyu, found that "for those earning over $5 million, the rate of departures spiked from 1.5% after the 2011 tax year to 2.125% after the 2012 tax year, with a similar effect among taxpayers earning $2–5 million in 2012."[96]

This spike is readily visible among filers who, immediately prior to the passage of Proposition 30, were in California's top income bracket under the new legislation for three straight years.

Even more striking, however, is Rauh and Shyu's finding that most of the wealth migration from California after Proposition 30 became law was due to wealthy people reporting less income, not fewer wealthy people paying taxes in California overall. Determining exactly why the wealthy reported less income due to Proposition 30 was beyond the scope of their paper, but the trends the paper identifies raise the specter of tax avoidance via the movement of capital assets out of state. Other possibilities cited by Rauh and Shyu include how Proposition 30 disincentivizes "engaging in wasteful rent-seeking activities" and causes "distortions of productive activity among California's most innovative residents."[97]

**Figure 10: Actual vs. predicted income of top-earning Californians after the passage of Proposition 30**[98]

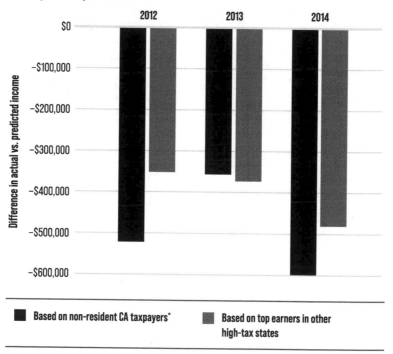

■ Based on non-resident CA taxpayers*      ▓ Based on top earners in other high-tax states

*Rauh and Shyu define non-resident California taxpayers as "taxpayers who do not reside in California, but file California non-resident returns, and who if California residents would have filed in the top California Proposition 30 created bracket from 2009–2011.

Regardless, observed drops in the incomes of wealthy California residents cannot be explained by similar drops in income among analogous residents of other states or non-resident filers. Rauh and Shyu compare tax returns of Californians subject to Proposition 30 to those of affluent filers in other high-tax states as well as those of California taxpayers who do not reside in the state. Regardless of the comparative metric, the average income deficit amounts to hundreds of thousands of dollars in each of the first three years in which Proposition 30 was in effect (see Figure 10). When taking into account that California has nearly 72,500 million-dollar earners, this income deficit amounts to tens of billions of dollars in vanished taxable economic activity.[99]

**Figure 11: Net AGI out-migration from California by top state income tax bracket in destination state, 2018[100]**

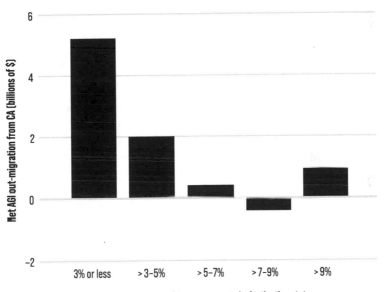

Rauh and Shyu also find that California's observed wealth flight is both "strongest in the direction of states with zero state taxes" and "concentrated among taxpayers who have filed in the top California bracket three years in a row."[101] These points are related because they both imply that tax savings are a big motivator of the wealthy to change residence. Thus, when Californians leave because of high income tax rates, they tend to settle in places with no state income tax at all, states like Florida, Washington, and Texas (see Figure 11). And even within the cohort of California taxpayers paying higher rates under Proposition 30, the wealthiest are the most likely to leave the state. The Tax Cuts and Jobs Act of 2017 has likely exacerbated this trend, given the cap it placed on state and local income tax deductions on federal income tax returns, which essentially removes a common work-around for the wealthy in high-tax states.[102]

## The Business Community Reacts

It's not just wealthy individuals who have opted to move out of California — it's also the businesses they own. This includes those of billionaire Elon Musk, once California's wealthiest resident. His announcement in December 2020 that he would be moving to Texas was foreshadowed by the construction of a gigantic factory for Tesla, Musk's electric car company, in Austin.[103] Tesla later announced that it will move its headquarters from California to Texas, a move that CNBC projected could save Musk billions of dollars in the long-term.[104]

The flight of firms and individuals such as Tesla and Elon Musk is illustrative of a long-standing problem that Proposition 30 has perpetuated. But it is not high corporate income taxes alone that are driving the exodus, as Texas, a popular destination for large firms fleeing California, has an even less competitive business tax climate when accounting for gross receipts taxes.[105] Proposition 30 is only a small piece of the harsh tax and regulatory puzzle in California, which is ranked #48 on Cato Institute's regulatory freedom index.[106]

Individual income taxes can also stifle business activity among pass-through entities such as sole proprietorships, which pay taxes via the personal returns of their owners. While sole proprietorships are by definition small businesses, in the right business climate, many have grown to become major national corporations, including Walmart, J.C. Penney, Kinko's, Ebay, and Marriott.[107] As of 2013, sole proprietorships generated some $150 billion in economic activity every quarter in California.[108] But as Elon Musk put it when discussing the construction of a Tesla factory in Texas, California "has a forest of redwoods and the little trees can't grow."

Meanwhile, various California business groups were notably tepid in their positions on Proposition 30. The California Chamber of Commerce stated that it didn't oppose the legislation "because the measure was supposed to be temporary and the state was in the midst of a dire financial situation."[109] But fast forward to 2016, when it was proposed to extend the income tax rates under Proposition 30, even in the midst of a booming economy, and this time the Chamber came out against the measure. But later, state records revealed that the opposition initiative garnered just $3,000 in campaign support, and some observers claimed that would-be individual donors were "afraid of retaliation from organized labor."[110] Rob Lapsley, president of the California Business Roundtable, opined that "business groups didn't think they could beat it," and were also "concerned about alternative tax proposals that would surface if [Proposition 30's extension] failed."[111] As a result, the 2016 ballot measure passed by a 27-point margin, whereas Proposition 30 originally passed by just an 11-point margin.[112]

In a recent report on why so many business headquarters have announced plans to relocate out of California in recent years, the Hoover Institution cited high individual income tax rates, due to their impact on pass-through entities such as S-corporations, LLC's, and limited partnerships.[113] This is an impact that the proposed surtax in Massachusetts is also likely to have if passed, and which we discuss in more detail in Chapter 6.

Finally, more concerning for California is that the Hoover Institution finds that the relocation trend appears to be accelerating in 2021, during the first six months of which the number of companies relocating exceeds the total for 2020. Though, as the report notes, business relocation planning can often take from one to three years "from the initiation of research to the announcement of the move," and in one instance cited by the Hoover Institution 12 years, likely placing at least some of the moves made or announced in 2021 on a timeline prior to the current pandemic and its attendant lockdowns. Therefore, it is not unreasonable to speculate that the dramatic increase in remote work in some industries in response to the pandemic has helped to lower barriers to exit for companies and contributed to the acceleration. We explore the possible impact that remote work, in relation to the proposed surtax, could have in Massachusetts in Chapter 6.

## Reductions in Tax Revenue

Thus, California state coffers became heavily reliant on revenue from wealthy taxpayers. Shortly before the law's passage, the California Legislative Analyst's Office estimated that over 78% of the tax revenue generated from Proposition 30 would come from the top 1% of income earners.[114] As of 2019, roughly 40% of all individual income tax revenue in California comes from filers with taxable income over $1 million.[115]

This reliance on the wealthy has left California extremely vulnerable to revenue volatility, tax avoidance efforts, and, more broadly, the whims of a small group of multi-billionaires. Thus, it's not surprising Rauh and Shyu's NBER paper found that "among top-bracket California taxpayers, outward migration and behavioral responses by stayers together eroded 45.2% of the windfall tax revenues from the reform within the first year and 60.9% within two years."[116]

It's worth noting that, for the most part, tax revenues from Proposition 30 have largely exceeded projections in recent years.[117] Possible explanations include high stock market performance, better-than-expected income gains among residents, or any of various poor assumptions made in the state's revenue models. However, this does not undermine the fact that, without the behavioral responses of the wealthy, California's state government would be billions of dollars richer.

Ultimately, Proposition 30 was passed to curb the need for further budget cuts in the aftermath of the Great Recession. However, the legislation has contributed to a tax and business environment that only increases the odds that California will face a budget deficit in a given year. Between 2008 and 2009, personal income tax revenue declined by 20.4% in California, while sales tax revenue declined by just 9.5%.[118] While sales taxes are undeniably regressive, an over-reliance on volatile income taxes often necessitates harsh budget cuts during a recession that hurt the poor the most at the time when they most need core services. Unfortunately, during the 2019–2020 budget cycle, California was slated to get 68.8% of general budget revenues from the personal income tax, and just 18.8% from sales taxes.[119] This imbalance of revenue sources is even more skewed towards the highly volatile personal income tax than in 2008–2009, when California got 52.2% of general budget revenues from the income tax and 26.6 from the sales tax.[120] If, in a future downturn, tax revenues fall significantly faster for personal income taxes than for sales taxes, as they did during the Great Recession, then California may be forced to reduce spending to balance its budget. Thus, the passage of Proposition 30 could create a future need for the kind of drastic cuts to social services that it was meant to prevent.

California's Proposition 30 has worsened the state's fiscal and economic situation by encouraging behavioral changes, such as wealth migration, with resultant tax revenue impacts that undermined the law's original purpose and weakened the state's economic resilience. However, California may have been luckier than most other states should they likewise adopt a similar tax scheme.

For wealthy individuals, it's relatively difficult to move outside California while remaining in the same labor market. By contrast, many eastern metropolises, notably New York, Boston, Philadelphia, and Washington, D.C., span several states. Thus, wealthy migrants could remain close to their jobs and social circles while still reaping windfall tax benefits.

As for corporations, especially in certain sectors, many of

them may be buoyed by the unique start-up culture of, say, Silicon Valley, or the proximity of ancillary business services and venues in a niche industry, like competitive surfing. Many other locations lack the industry specialization necessary to maintain a healthy business climate without competitive tax rates.

It's also the case that, in some states, personal income tax revenues tend to be even more unreliable than those of California. Arizona is an ironic example, given that it just voted to place a 3.5% surcharge on its highest income tax bracket in November 2020.[121] From 2008 to 2009, its income tax revenues plunged 24.4%, the steepest drop in the country.[122]

While state budget deficits after COVID-19 have not been nearly as great as first feared, Proposition 30 has prompted disinvestment from wealthy individuals and corporations. Now it's up to California whether it wants to repeat the mistakes of the post-Great Recession recovery, or start to build a more sustainable tax system for everyone.

But the lessons to be drawn from California are not just in terms of the potential impact on the Commonwealth's budget and economy. In both California and Massachusetts, the increases in income tax rates for high-income individuals have been tied to increases in funding for specific purposes, namely education (in California) and education and transportation (in Massachusetts). We must also consider whether our elected officials will keep their commitment to spend the money on their stated priorities. It is that subject to which we turn in the next chapter.

Chapter 2

# Public Privilege

## The Shell Game to Fill the General Fund

The Massachusetts Constitution has authorized an income tax since 1915. Ever since, that taxing authority has always been subject to one significant restraint: a prohibition on graduated tax rates. Put another way, our Constitution requires a flat income tax. Currently, that flat income tax rate sits at 5%, a competitive rate that serves the Commonwealth well in its fight for good jobs against high tax jurisdictions such as New York, Connecticut, and California. Indeed, despite the Commonwealth's past reputation as "Taxachusetts," on five occasions voters have been asked to amend the constitution to eliminate the ban on graduated income taxes (in 1962, 1968, 1972, 1976, and 1994) — and they've rejected the pitch every time.[123]

In the run-up to the 2018 election cycle, proponents of graduated income taxes thought they had found a solution to the unpopularity of their cause: assure voters that any money raised by a tax hike would be earmarked for two priorities popular with the middle class: public education and transportation. Thus, in their push for a graduated income tax or so-called "Fair Share Amendment," tax hike proponents linked a 4% rate hike on incomes over $1 million to a constitutional earmark of the money to education and transportation spending. Specifically, the proposed graduated income tax ballot measure stated:

> To provide the resources for quality public education and affordable public colleges and universities, and for the repair and maintenance of roads, bridges and public transportation, all revenues received in accordance with this paragraph shall be expended, subject to appropriation, only for these purposes. In addition to

the taxes on income otherwise authorized under this Article, there shall be an additional tax of 4 percent on that portion of annual taxable income in excess of $1,000,000 (one million dollars) reported on any return related to those taxes.[124]

The proposed ballot measure never made it before voters. In June 2018, in the landmark decision *Anderson v. Healey*, the Massachusetts Supreme Judicial Court ruled that the measure violated the state constitution's ban on citizen-initiated ballot questions that combine unrelated subject matters—in that case, a new graduated income tax and two disparate subjects of spending.

But the related subject matter requirement does not apply to proposed constitutional amendments that originate in the legislature. So almost as soon as the ink was dry on *Anderson*, supporters of the tax hike on Beacon Hill moved the graduated income tax into a legislatively-proposed constitutional amendment and set the stage for a renewed battle in 2022. Their expectation remains that voters, eager to support increased education and transportation spending, will vote for the tax increase.

But that raises a crucial question: if voters go for it, will the graduated income tax actually lead to increased education and transportation spending? In this chapter, we attempt to answer the question from two different angles. First, we look at the amendment's language and, just as importantly, the language used in the legal arguments made in support of the amendment when it was challenged as a citizen-initiated petition prior to the 2018 election. Second, we turn again to California, where Proposition 30 raised the highest income tax bracket in the state to 13.3%. Proposition 30 was adopted with a similar understanding that additional revenues raised by the tax increase would be earmarked specifically for K–12 education and funding for community colleges.

### The "Fair Share" Amendment

Proponents of the amendment to institute a graduated income tax in Massachusetts, beginning with a 4% surtax for incomes above $1 million, certainly want voters to think that the revenue it raises will lead to increased education and transportation spending. Raise Up Massachusetts, the coalition of powerful labor unions and other advocacy groups that originally developed the proposal, states unambiguously on its website that "the new revenue, approximately $2 billion a year, would be spent on quality public education, affordable public colleges and universities, and the repair and maintenance of roads, bridges, and public transportation." It suggests that this "new revenue" will be used to "improve" schools and to "invest" in transportation.[125]

Maybe. Or maybe not. The fact is, the proposed constitutional amendment contains no assurance of new spending on education or transportation. To the contrary, it is entirely possible that even as tax revenues increase, education and transportation spending could stay the same, or even fall, without violating the amendment.

The critical point is this: on its face, the proposed amendment only requires that the specific revenue raised by the tax be earmarked to education and transportation. It says nothing about the total amount spent on those two priorities. And money, of course, is fungible.

Some simple math shows the problem. The new tax, as of 2018, was expected to raise about $2 billion each year. How much does the state government already spend on education and transportation? The fiscal year 2020 budget directed $7.9 billion to the Executive Office of Education and $573 million to the Department of Transportation, together almost $8.5 billion, all funded from sources other than the graduated income tax.[126]

If the constitutional amendment passes, the legislature could play a shell game: dedicate the $2 billion raised through the graduated income tax to those two line items, add $6.5 billion in revenue from other sources—down from the $8.5 billion previously being used—and leave total education and transportation spending exactly where they were. In the meantime, the legislature will have freed up $2 billion in revenue from other sources to spend on whatever it wants.

Is that really how it would work? Just ask Attorney General

Maura Healey. In *Anderson v. Healey*, the primary legal problem
with the proposed ballot measure was its dedication of the expected graduated income tax revenue to education and transportation spending; that sort of "specific appropriation," cemented
in the constitution, cannot be done in a citizen-initiated ballot
measure. In attempting to address this hurdle, the Attorney General's brief urged the Supreme Judicial Court not to worry about
it, because any earmarking could be rendered moot by precisely
the sort of shell game described above:

> The Legislature would retain ultimate discretion over spending
> choices for the additional reason that money is fungible. Because
> the proposed amendment does not require otherwise, the Legisla-
> ture could choose to reduce funding in specified budget categories
> from other sources and replace it with the new surtax revenue. As
> long as the total spending in these combined categories did not
> fall below the revenue generated by the surtax in any particular
> year, the Legislature would be in compliance with the proposed
> amendment.[127]

The late Chief Justice Ralph Gants understood this too, asking the Attorney General's counsel at oral argument whether she
agreed that, if the graduated income tax amendment passed, it
"may or may not result in any increase in education or transportation or education spending." *(sic)* Counsel responded that the
Chief Justice's understanding was correct.[128]

Tax hike proponents on Beacon Hill also recognize that
the graduated income tax measure contains no assurance of
increased education and transportation spending. And they
see no problem with it. During floor debates on the proposed
legislature-initiated ballot measure, an amendment was offered
that would have required the new tax revenues to be spent incrementally on education and transportation, over and above what
already is spent. That amendment was overwhelmingly defeated,
leaving legislative budget writers maximum discretion to engage
in the shell game predicted in the Attorney General's brief.

## California's Fiscal Gymnastics

In its opinion in *Anderson v. Healey*, the Massachusetts Supreme Judicial Court wrote: "We are not entirely unaware of the possibility that, as the plaintiffs argue, these 'broad areas of public concern' [i.e. funding for education and transportation] were added to the initiative petition as a means to 'sweeten the pot' for voters."

The strategy of "sweetening the pot" for voters on initiative petitions, as noted by the SJC, was used successfully in California when voters approved Proposition 30 on November 6, 2012. As noted in the previous chapter, Proposition 30 proposed a temporary (seven-year) income tax hike for high-income individuals, with revenues dedicated to K–12 education and community colleges. Voters approved Proposition 30 by a margin of 55.4% to 44.6%.[129] Proposition 30 increased income taxes on single filers in California to the highest in the nation, including imposing a 13.3% marginal tax rate on income over $1 million—an increase of 29.1% over the previous "millionaires tax" rate of 10.3%.[130] Voters later extended the income tax hike for another 12 years when they approved Proposition 55 on November 8, 2016.[131]

The promised bounty did not arrive. A review of the record in California makes clear that since the passage of Proposition 30, the state has funded K–12 education and community colleges at or near the minimum funding amounts previously established by a much older constitutional initiative petition, Proposition 98 (1988).

Proposition 98 uses a complicated series of formulas to establish a minimum amount of the state's revenues that must be allocated to education in a given year. According to the California Legislative Analyst's Office (LAO), the constitutional minimum funding level has closely defined actual appropriations by the legislature: "Although the state can provide more funding than required, in practice it usually funds at or near the guarantee."[132]

Kevin Gordon, a California policy consultant and expert on Prop 98, says that "as soon as [the legislation] got implemented, the legislature was always trying to figure out,- what does it take just to do the minimum—and once they do the minimum, check the box, we're done. And that's what happened: it became a funding cap instead of a funding floor."[133]

In the 2012 voter guide for Proposition 30, proponents said: "The money raised for schools is directed into a special fund the legislature can't touch and can't be used for state bureaucracy." Opponents said "it allows the politicians to take money currently earmarked for education and spend it on other programs. We'll never know where the money really goes."[134]

Figure 1. Proposition 98 share of California general fund revenues (millions of $) and applicable funding test (FY13–FY21)[135]

| Fiscal Year | Total General Fund Revenues | Prop 98 share of General Fund Revenues | Prop 98 share as % of General Fund Revenues | Applicable funding requirement |
|---|---|---|---|---|
| 2012-13 | $96,447 | $41,799 | 40.90% | Test 1 |
| 2013-14 | $101,838 | $43,145 | 42.40% | Test 2 |
| 2014-15 | $113,356 | $50,011 | 44.10% | Test 1 |
| 2015-16 | $119,975 | $49,433 | 41.20% | Test 3 |
| 2016-17 | $122,054 | $50,240 | 41.20% | Test 3 |
| 2017-18 | $132,827 | $52,951 | 39.90% | Test 1 |
| 2018-19 | $142,912 | $54,746 | 38.30% | Test 1 |
| 2019-20 | $139,745 | $54,470 | 39.00% | Test 1 |
| 2020-21 | $153,594 | $56,942 | 37.10% | Test 1 |
| TOTAL | $1,122,748 | $453,737 | 40.40% | |

With the benefit of hindsight, it is easy to determine the extent to which proponents and opponents were correct in their assessments. The answer is that proponents were technically right in saying that the revenue from the income tax hike for K–12 and community colleges would be put in a special fund dedicated exclusively to those programs. But the opponents were also right in saying that Proposition 30 funds could be spent on other programs for the same reason stated by the Attorney General in Massachusetts to the SJC in relation to the surtax proposal. In California, the legislature applied Proposition 30 funds to K–12 and community colleges to the minimum funding requirements of Proposition 98. This replacement effectively freed up state funds that otherwise would have been obligated to minimum funding. Given that Proposition 98 effectively established the annual funding levels for K–12 and community colleges in California, one might expect that revenues from Proposition 30 would be used to increase funding above the minimum level. In fact, about 40% of Proposition 30 revenues have gone to K–12 and community colleges, but about 60% have not. In 2019–20, for example, Test 1 of Proposition 98 was operative, guaranteeing that K–12 and community colleges would receive a fixed share (about 40%) of state General Fund revenue.[136] Because Proposition 98 minimum funding in 2019–20 was based on total state revenue and because Proposition 30 revenues were included in total state revenue, approximately 40% of Proposition 30 revenues likewise went to K–12 and community colleges. The rest effectively went to the General Fund.

Figure 2. Percentage of Prop 98 Minimum funding (millions of $) provided (2013–21)[137]

| Fiscal Year | Prop 98 Minimum Guarantee | Prop 98 funding from General Fund | Prop 98 funding from Local Property Tax | Actual Prop 98 funding – Total | Percentage of Prop 98 Minimum funding provided |
|---|---|---|---|---|---|
| 2013 | $57,888 | $41,799 | $16,297 | $58,096 | 100.36% |
| 2014 | $59,041 | $43,145 | $15,896 | $59,041 | 100.00% |
| 2015 | $67,125 | $50,011 | $17,114 | $67,125 | 100.00% |
| 2016 | $68,942 | $49,433 | $19,679 | $69,112 | 100.25% |
| 2017 | $71,643 | $50,240 | $21,403 | $71,643 | 100.00% |
| 2018 | $75,459 | $52,951 | $22,625 | $75,576 | 100.15% |
| 2019 | $78,522 | $54,746 | $23,776 | $78,522 | 100.00% |
| 2020 | $79,544 | $54,470 | $25,073 | $79,544 | 100.00% |
| 2021 | $82,828 | $56,942 | $25,887 | $82,828 | 100.00% |
| TOTAL | $640,992 | $453,737 | $187,750 | $641,488 | 100.08% |

Total funding of Proposition 98 in the nine year period from FY2013 to FY2021, including funding from local property taxes and state general funds, was $641.488 billion. This is 0.08% more than the Proposition 98 constitutional minimum requirement of $640.992 billion over this period, as shown in Figure 2.

In the nine-year period from FY2013 to FY2021, California collected $61.259 billion in tax revenues from Proposition 30 and deposited the funds into the Education Protection Account for K–12 schools and community colleges, as required by Proposition 30. Over this same period, Proposition 98 required that 40.4% of total state revenues be appropriated for K–12 schools and community colleges. Because of this requirement, Proposition 30 revenues had the effect of increasing the preexisting Proposition 98 minimum funding requirement by $28.348 billion over this period, i.e. 40.4% of $61.259 billion.

**Figure 3. Proposition 30 revenues (millions of $) used to replace General Funds (FY13–21)[138]**

| Fiscal Year | Prop 30 revenues | Prop 98 share of General Fund Revenues | Amount that Prop 30 increased Prop 98 minimum funding | Prop 30 revenues used to replace General Funds |
|---|---|---|---|---|
| 2013 | $7,314 | 40.9% | $2,995 | $4,319 |
| 2014 | $7,061 | 42.4% | $2,992 | $4,069 |
| 2015 | $8,712 | 44.1% | $3,844 | $4,868 |
| 2016 | $8,092 | 41.2% | $3,334 | $4,758 |
| 2017 | $7,538 | 41.2% | $3,103 | $4,435 |
| 2018 | $6,809 | 39.9% | $2,714 | $4,095 |
| 2019 | $7,697 | 38.3% | $2,949 | $4,748 |
| 2010 | $8,036 | 39.0% | $3,132 | $4,904 |
| 2021 | $8,887 | 37.1% | $3,295 | $5,592 |
| TOTAL | $70,146 | 40.4% | $28,348 | $41,798 |

The 59.6% balance of the $61.259 billion in revenues from Proposition 30 that were deposited into the Education Protection Account amounts to $41.798 billion. Essentially, this money reduced the amount of preexisting revenues that the state legislature had to appropriate for K–12 and community colleges from state general funds. Thus $41.798 billion of the $61.259 billion in Proposition 30 tax revenue collected over this period and deposited into the Education Protection Account, i.e., the amount in

excess of the 40.4% Proposition 98 minimum requirement, had the direct effect of freeing up $41.798 billion in general funds that the state legislature was able to use for any other purposes that it chose. This is demonstrated in Figure 3.

The mechanism demonstrated in Figure 3, i.e. replacing funding in specified budget categories with new surtax revenue, could happen in Massachusetts, but without even the restraint provided by Prop 98. At least in California, the state legislature was able to use only 59.6% of revenues from a dedicated tax increase for other purposes. In Massachusetts, 100% of revenue from the proposed graduated surtax, ostensibly dedicated to funding of transportation and education, could be used for any purpose that the legislature may choose.

### A Spending Glut Elsewhere

The infusion of discretionary revenue from Proposition 30 has allowed the California state Legislature to increase spending in other areas. Figure 4 shows that state government employment increased by 10.6% between FY2013, when Proposition 30 passed, and FY2020. During the same period, Massachusetts' state payroll grew by just 0.3%. On average, other states added 1.8% over that time, according to data published by the federal Bureau of Labor Statistics.[139]

Figure 4. Percent increase in state government employment (FY13-FY20)[140]

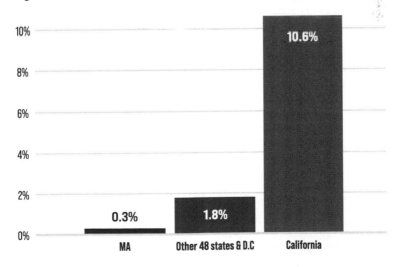

Over the same FY2013 to FY2020 period, state government payroll, which excludes teachers, grew by 50.3% in California and by 24.0% in Massachusetts, as shown in Figure 5.[141] The payrolls of the other 48 states and the District of Columbia grew by 24.4%.

Figure 5. Percent increase in state government wages (FY13-FY20)[142]

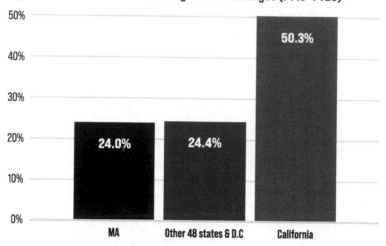

Figure 6. Change in California K-12 public school students, teachers, and instructional staff after Proposition 30[143]

| | 2013-2014 | 2019-2020 | Difference | Percent Difference |
|---|---|---|---|---|
| Public school enrollment | 6,236,672 | 6,415,254 | 178,582 | 2.9% |
| Number of teachers | 292,505 | 293,619 | 1,114 | 0.4% |
| Number of instructional staff | 333,766 | 374,003 | 40,237 | 12.1% |
| Enrolled students per teacher | 21.3 | 21.8 | 0.5 | 2.3% |
| Enrolled students per instructional staff | 18.7 | 17.2 | -1.5 | -8.0% |
| State rank - enrolled students per teacher | 48 | 51 | -3 | N/A |
| State rank - enrolled students per instructional staff | 49 | 50 | -1 | N/A |

Despite the funding increase that was ostensibly meant to provide for K–12 schools, California's student-teacher ratio has actually risen since Proposition 30 passed, according to data published by the National Education Association.[144] In 2013, prior to its passage, California ranked 48th out of the 50 states and D.C. in enrolled students per teacher. By 2019, its ranking had fallen to 51st, the worst in the nation. The same trend occurred in enrolled students per instructional staff, including teachers and related direct education providers. California ranked 49th in the nation in this regard in the fall of 2013. In the fall of 2019, it had fallen to 50th, behind only Utah, as shown in Figures 6 and 7.

Revenue from Proposition 30 has helped facilitate sizable pay raises and increased retirement and health contributions for employees of California state departments. In FY2019, California's expenditures for wages, retirement contributions, and health care contributions were $8.2 billion higher than they were in FY2013 before voters approved Proposition 30, according to data published by the State Controller.[145] In FY2019, Proposition 30 generated less than that, $7.7 billion, in tax revenue.

**Figure 7. NEA state rankings of enrolled students per teacher and instructional staff (Fall 2013–Fall 2019)[146]**

| | Enrolled students per teacher | | | | Enrolled students per instructional staff | | | |
|---|---|---|---|---|---|---|---|---|
| State | 2013 | Rank 2013 | 2019 | Rank 2019 | Fall 2013 | Rank 2013 | Fall 2019 | Rank 2019 |
| Alabama | 15.9 | 34 | 15.6 | 32 | 13.8 | 33 | 13.5 | 35 |
| Alaska | 16.2 | 38 | 17.0 | 42 | 14.5 | 41 | 15.6 | 45 |
| Arizona | 18.2 | 45 | 17.5 | 43 | 16.7 | 45 | 16.1 | 47 |
| Arkansas | 15.2 | 26 | 14.8 | 24 | 13.1 | 28 | 12.8 | 26 |
| California | 21.3 | 48 | 21.8 | 51 | 18.7 | 49 | 17.2 | 50 |
| Colorado | 15.4 | 31 | 15.8 | 35 | 13.0 | 25 | 12.9 | 27 |
| Connecticut | 13.0 | 11 | 12.6 | 8 | 10.3 | 3 | 10.2 | 5 |
| Delaware | 14.7 | 22 | 14.6 | 21 | 13.1 | 27 | 13.1 | 33 |
| D.C | 12.3 | 6 | 12.9 | 11 | 10.9 | 7 | 11.4 | 12 |

| State | Enrolled students per teacher | | | | Enrolled students per instructional staff | | | |
|---|---|---|---|---|---|---|---|---|
| | 2013 | Rank 2013 | 2019 | Rank 2019 | Fall 2013 | Rank 2013 | Fall 2019 | Rank 2019 |
| Florida | 16.0 | 35 | 20.0 | 48 | 14.6 | 42 | 14.6 | 41 |
| Georgia | 15.8 | 33 | 15.1 | 28 | 13.7 | 32 | 12.9 | 30 |
| Hawaii | 16.7 | 41 | 15.9 | 36 | 14.4 | 39 | 13.7 | 36 |
| Idaho | 19.8 | 47 | 18.5 | 46 | 17.7 | 47 | 16.1 | 46 |
| Illinois | 16.1 | 37 | 15.3 | 30 | 14.4 | 40 | 11.2 | 10 |
| Indiana | 17.1 | 42 | 16.9 | 41 | 14.9 | 43 | 14.7 | 42 |
| Iowa | 14.3 | 19 | 13.7 | 15 | 12.4 | 17 | 11.8 | 15 |
| Kansas | 14.1 | 17 | 13.9 | 17 | 12.6 | 20 | 12.3 | 21 |
| Kentucky | 16.5 | 40 | 16.3 | 40 | 14.4 | 38 | 14.1 | 38 |
| Louisiana | 16.0 | 36 | 15.0 | 25 | 12.9 | 23 | 11.8 | 14 |
| Maine | 12.1 | 5 | 12.5 | 6 | 10.3 | 4 | 10.6 | 8 |
| Maryland | 14.6 | 20 | 14.7 | 22 | 11.9 | 12 | 11.9 | 16 |
| Massachusetts | 13.5 | 15 | 12.7 | 9 | 12.0 | 13 | 10.9 | 9 |
| Michigan | 22.6 | 51 | 17.7 | 45 | 18.6 | 48 | 14.9 | 43 |
| Minnesota | 15.6 | 32 | 16.2 | 37 | 14.3 | 37 | 14.6 | 40 |
| Mississippi | 15.2 | 27 | 14.7 | 23 | 13.6 | 31 | 12.9 | 28 |
| Missouri | 13.5 | 14 | 11.6 | 5 | 12.0 | 14 | 10.3 | 6 |
| Montana | 13.3 | 12 | 13.9 | 18 | 11.6 | 11 | 12.1 | 17 |
| Nebraska | 13.0 | 10 | 13.6 | 14 | 11.5 | 10 | 12.1 | 18 |
| Nevada | 17.9 | 44 | 20.8 | 49 | 15.1 | 44 | 16.8 | 48 |
| New Hampshire | 11.9 | 3 | 10.4 | 1 | 9.5 | 2 | 9.8 | 4 |
| New Jersey | 11.8 | 2 | 11.6 | 4 | 11.0 | 8 | 9.5 | 2 |
| New Mexico | 15.1 | 24 | 15.6 | 33 | 13.5 | 29 | 14.0 | 37 |
| New York | 12.8 | 9 | 12.9 | 10 | 12.0 | 15 | 11.5 | 13 |
| North Carolina | 15.2 | 25 | 15.1 | 26 | 13.0 | 26 | 12.9 | 29 |
| North Dakota | 12.1 | 4 | 11.0 | 3 | 10.4 | 5 | 9.6 | 3 |
| Ohio | 17.2 | 43 | 15.7 | 34 | 14.0 | 36 | 12.3 | 20 |
| Oklahoma | 16.2 | 39 | 16.3 | 39 | 13.8 | 34 | 14.2 | 39 |
| Oregon | 21.5 | 49 | 19.4 | 47 | 19.1 | 50 | 17.0 | 49 |

| State | Enrolled students per teacher | | | | Enrolled students per instructional staff | | | |
|---|---|---|---|---|---|---|---|---|
| | 2013 | Rank 2013 | 2019 | Rank 2019 | Fall 2013 | Rank 2013 | Fall 2019 | Rank 2019 |
| Pennsylvania | 14.6 | 21 | 14.1 | 20 | 12.7 | 22 | 12.4 | 23 |
| Rhode Island | 13.4 | 13 | 13.1 | 12 | 12.2 | 16 | 11.3 | 11 |
| South Carolina | 15.3 | 28 | 15.2 | 29 | 13.0 | 24 | 12.7 | 25 |
| South Dakota | 13.8 | 16 | 13.8 | 16 | 12.4 | 18 | 12.6 | 24 |
| Tennessee | 15.0 | 23 | 16.2 | 38 | 12.7 | 21 | 13.1 | 32 |
| Texas | 15.3 | 29 | 15.1 | 27 | 13.6 | 30 | 13.1 | 34 |
| Utah | 22.5 | 50 | 21.5 | 50 | 19.3 | 51 | 17.3 | 51 |
| Vermont | 10.0 | 1 | 10.5 | 2 | 8.2 | 1 | 9.1 | 1 |
| Virginia | 12.5 | 8 | 12.5 | 7 | 10.8 | 6 | 10.6 | 7 |
| Washington | 19.4 | 46 | 17.6 | 44 | 17.2 | 46 | 15.5 | 44 |
| West Virginia | 14.3 | 18 | 14.0 | 19 | 12.5 | 19 | 12.1 | 19 |
| Wisconsin | 15.4 | 30 | 15.6 | 31 | 14.0 | 35 | 13.0 | 31 |
| Wyoming | 12.4 | 7 | 13.5 | 13 | 11.1 | 9 | 12.3 | 22 |
| United States | 15.9 | | 15.7 | | 13.9 | | 13.2 | |

Figure 8. Change in California state employee wages, retirement benefits, and health benefits (2013-19)[147]

| State Departments | Employees | Total Wages | Total Retirement & Health Contribution | Total Wages, Retirement & Health Contribution |
|---|---|---|---|---|
| 2019 | 255,380 | $19,138,635,937 | $8,944,171,442 | $28,082,807,379 |
| 2013 | 235,249 | $14,613,713,360 | $5,244,670,686 | $19,858,384,046 |
| Increase/ decrease | 20,131 | $4,524,922,577 | $3,699,500,756 | $8,224,423,333 |
| Increase/ decrease % | 8.6% | 31.0% | 70.5% | 41.4% |

The proposed constitutional amendment to institute a 4% surtax on annual income over $1 million in Massachusetts is being marketed by proponents as a means to collect between $1.6 and $2.2 billion per year that is critically needed for transportation and education.[148] But in 2018 counsel for the Massachusetts Attorney General told the Massachusetts Supreme Judicial Court the opposite could be true when they wrote in the state's brief that "because the proposed amendment does not require otherwise, the Legislature could choose to reduce funding in specified budget categories [i.e. education and transportation] from other sources and replace it with the new surtax revenue... As long as total spending in these combined categories did not fall below the revenue generated by the surtax in any particular year, the Legislature would be in compliance with the proposed amendment."[149] It would remain solely to the discretion of the legislature whether it would adhere to the spirit of the amendment. By exactly the means described by the Attorney General's office, the legislature would be authorized effectively to spend all of the expected tax revenue on anything it desires.

In California, that is essentially what happened after voters approved Proposition 30 in 2012, forming the highest marginal state individual income tax rate in the nation. Proposition 30 created what in essence is a $41.8 billion discretionary fund that the state legislature could spend on whatever it chose. In part because of Proposition 30, California's state employee payroll increased by more than twice the national average between FY2013 and FY2020.[150]

The proposed Massachusetts graduated tax surcharge is a close cousin to California's Proposition 30. The selling point of both proposals is that the new funds would be used for specific purposes. It's up to voters to decide whether these ostensible earmarks "sweeten the pot" enough, or whether there's a better way to guarantee funding to core services. When advocates tell you that the funds from the surtax will be used for education and transportation and not to pad the state bureaucracy, be warned. Padding bureaucracy is the likely outcome.

To put that outcome in context, we look in the next section at the public payroll figures for Massachusetts during the pandemic and compare them with the state's private-sector employment numbers.

## Holding the Public Sector Harmless During the Pandemic

In April 2020, one month after the start of COVID-19 lockdowns in the United States, the national unemployment rate hit a record high 14.8%. This jarring milestone arrived on the heels of the 20-year low 3.5% unemployment recorded just a few months earlier, in January 2020.[151]

By the time Congress passed its first coronavirus stimulus package in May 2020, an astonishing 36 million Americans had lost their jobs as a consequence of lockdowns and the reduced economic activity stemming from fears of the virus.[152] As of January 2021, when Congress resumed negotiations over its third coronavirus stimulus legislation, the national unemployment rate had dropped back down to 6.3%.[153] But how did Massachusetts state employees fare during the crisis?

### The Public and Private Sectors Diverge

The bleak economic state created by the tumult of 2020 has made responsible governance and the astute allocation of resources even more important. While there was a minor decrease of 1.6% in the total number of employees on Massachusetts' state payroll from February through December 2020, total employment in the Commonwealth experienced a dramatic 9.2% plunge during this period.[154]

The state reported 93,185 employees on its January 16, 2021 payrolls, a decrease of just 1.7% from the 94,763 recorded on February 29, 2020, just as the pandemic was starting.[155] These statistics are particularly striking because unemployment in Massachusetts surpassed all other states with a high of 16.1% in July 2020.[156]

A glance at total nonfarm employment numbers across Massachusetts — encompassing both the public and private sector — explains the dramatic surge in unemployment by the summer of 2020.[157]

Total state employment was at a 30-year high in January 2020, with 3,729,900 employees.[158] This number, the result of a decade of steadily climbing employment, represented a 17.8%

increase from the 3,166,200 recorded at the nadir of the Great Recession in November 2009.[159]

By March 2020, total employment in Massachusetts had dipped slightly to 3,665,000 before swiftly nose diving in April 2020 to 2,853,900, a 23.5% decrease from the January 2020 peak.[160] One month of the policies instituted to combat the COVID-19 pandemic, along with residents' fears of transmission, brought Massachusetts to its lowest employment levels since 1992.[161]

The state payroll, however, did not suffer from the April plunge. It maintained its February 2020 employment levels, with 94,775 employees recorded for April 25, 2020.[162]

Following the historically low totals of April 2020, statewide employment climbed sharply as the state relaxed its lockdown mandates in summer. By September 2020, nearly 541,100 individuals had re-entered the workforce, although this growth reversed in subsequent months as lockdown restrictions tightened again.[163] Employment in the state declined by 8,400 individuals between September and December 2020.[164]

These trends largely did not bear out in the state payroll. Most state departments experienced minimal, if any, decrease in employment numbers from March 2020 to April 2020. Comparing numbers from February 2020 to January 2021, however, shows a slight drop in employment in certain departments.

Most notable among these are Bridgewater State University (5.2% decrease), UMass System (4.4% decrease), Sheriff Department of Plymouth (4.3% decrease), and Department of Correction (2.9% decrease).[165] By comparison, some of the Massachusetts non-farm industries that experienced the greatest reduction in employment over the 12-month period ending in December 2020 were Leisure & Hospitality (38.4% decrease), Other Services (18.7%) and Education & Health Services (8.1%).[166]

Other state departments, meanwhile, reported increased employment during the same nine-month period. The number of individuals employed by the Department of Public Health grew by 4.6% — an expected response during a pandemic—while the

Department of Children and Families and Massachusetts Bay Transportation Authority increased their respective workforces by 1.1% and 0.9%.[167] The graph below spotlights employment trends for the Massachusetts state departments that experienced the greatest fluctuation since the start of the pandemic.

The emergence of these disparities between state payroll and total state employment trends throughout such a trying year elicits moral enquiries with no simple answers. For instance, to what extent should taxpayers not employed by the Commonwealth, who comprise 97.2% of the Massachusetts workforce, subsidize workers on the state payroll (2.8% of the workforce) in the face of such economic realities?[168]

**Figure 9: State Government v. All MA Workers Employment During the Covid-19 Pandemic**

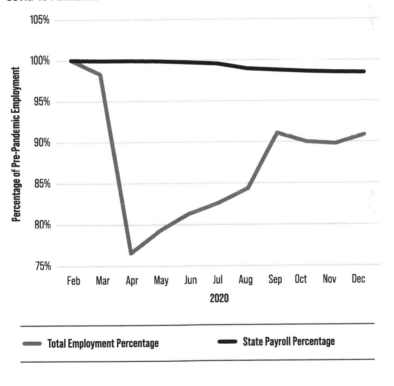

## Figure 10: Employment Across Select MA State Departments, Feb 2020 Through Jan 2021

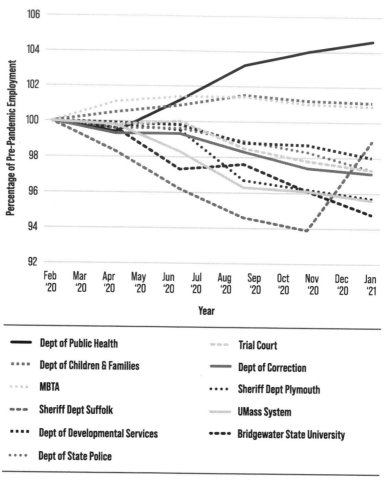

Legend:
- **Dept of Public Health**
- **Dept of Children & Families**
- **MBTA**
- **Sheriff Dept Suffolk**
- **Dept of Developmental Services**
- **Dept of State Police**
- **Trial Court**
- **Dept of Correction**
- **Sheriff Dept Plymouth**
- **UMass System**
- **Bridgewater State University**

Reviewing employment trends across Massachusetts throughout 2020, from the 30-year high in January to the 28-year low in April, reveals that state employees remained largely shielded from the dramatic fluctuations experienced by employees not on the state payroll. Meanwhile, over the 12-month period ended on January 27, 2021, the number of small businesses open in Massachusetts had decreased by 37.7%.[169] The combined effects of lockdowns and consumer fears are among the primary contributors to the swings in private sector employment.

While much of the private sector has yet to fully recoup the jobs lost during the pandemic's economic fallout, the state payroll, as we note, has remained largely unaffected. The number of state employees declined by 1.7% from February 2020 to January 2021, even while total employment in the Commonwealth dropped by 9.2% from January 2020 through December 2020.

While the economy has improved since December 2020, this discrepancy brings up the larger issue of whether the largely unscathed state government also should have pulled back on costs during the downturn, given that its revenues come largely from the weakened private sector. And it is perhaps more important to consider this question now, given the budget shell game even proponents of the proposed tax amendment admit is possible, and likewise given the evidence that California's experience offers showing precisely how the State Assembly played the game to bloat the Golden State's public payroll.

As the graduated income tax amendment goes to the ballot in November 2022, whether to prioritize a market led recovery from COVID or an expansion of public-sector investment will be a subject of substantial debate. Indeed, the proposed 4% surcharge would give Massachusetts the grim distinction of having the highest short-term capital gains tax rate of any state in the nation, potentially impacting private-sector growth. We explain this in the next chapter.

Chapter 3

# Making Massachusetts Less Economically Competitive

## A Decision to Decimate the Financial Services Sector in Massachusetts

As noted earlier, the graduated income tax proposal would create a 4% surtax on personal annual income of more than $1 million over and above the current state income tax rate of 5% for all filers. For filers who have total income greater than $1 million and short-term capital gains, the amount representing short-term capital gains in excess of total income would effectively be taxed at 16% rather than at the current rate of 12%, giving Massachusetts the highest short-term capital gains rate in the country. Meanwhile, Massachusetts' long-term capital gains tax rate would be the highest in New England.[170] Both could be especially damaging to the Commonwealth's financial services industry, a major employer in the state and ultimately a driver of economic activity in many other sectors. If Massachusetts hopes to have a market-led recovery, such high capital gains tax rates, both short-term and long-term, would represent significant barriers to achieving that goal.

### Curbing Investment, Squandering Opportunity

Research shows that higher taxes on capital gains hamper investment, reduce productivity, and ultimately slow down wage growth.[171] Nobel laureate Robert Lucas estimates that if the U.S. eliminated its capital gains and dividend taxes, the capital stock of American plants and equipment would be 50% larger.[172]

## Figure 1. Top Marginal Short-Term Capital Gains Tax Rate by State, 2015[173]

| State | State rate | State | State rate |
|---|---|---|---|
| Massachusetts (if GIT passes) | 16.0% | Oklahoma | 5.3% |
| California | 13.3% | Mississippi | 5.0% |
| Massachusetts (current) | 12.0% | Utah | 5.0% |
| New York | 8.8% | Montana | 6.9% |
| Oregon | 9.9% | Louisiana | 6.0% |
| Minnesota | 9.9% | Kansas | 4.8% |
| New Jersey | 9.0% | Arkansas | 7.0% |
| Vermont | 9.0% | Colorado | 4.6% |
| Washington, D.C. | 9.0% | Indiana | 3.3% |
| Maryland | 5.8% | Arizona | 4.5% |
| Maine | 8.0% | Michigan | 4.3% |
| Iowa | 9.0% | Alabama | 5.0% |
| Hawaii | 7.3% | South Carolina | 7.0% |
| Idaho | 7.4% | Illinois | 3.8% |
| Nebraska | 6.8% | Pennsylvania | 3.1% |
| Connecticut | 6.7% | New Mexico | 4.9% |
| Delaware | 6.6% | North Dakota | 3.2% |
| West Virginia | 6.5% | Alaska | 0.0% |
| Rhode Island | 6.0% | Florida | 0.0% |
| Georgia | 6.0% | Nevada | 0.0% |
| Missouri | 6.0% | New Hampshire | 0.0% |
| Kentucky | 6.0% | South Dakota | 0.0% |
| Virginia | 5.8% | Tennessee | 0.0% |
| North Carolina | 5.8% | Texas | 0.0% |
| Ohio | 5.3% | Washington | 0.0% |
| Wisconsin | 7.7% | Wyoming | 0.0% |

Further, Massachusetts is already considered one of the least appealing states in the country for day trading, as it is the only state that taxes short-term capital gains at a consistently higher rate than long-term capital gains.[174] And though one may not be tempted to shed tears for day-traders, impacts to the financial services industry ultimately have broad economic consequences.

**Figure 2: Correlation Between Average Capital Gains of High Income Earners and Top Marginal Capital Gains Tax Rate by State, 2018[175]**

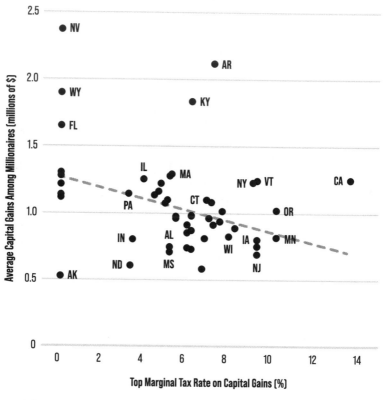

The Massachusetts Technology Collaborative has made it clear that venture capital has been a crucial enabler of the recent growth in small tech and healthcare startups in Massachusetts.[176] In 2018 alone, private equity firms invested more than $10.4 billion in innovative Massachusetts companies, constituting almost 2% of the state's GDP that year.[177] Research has shown that one new "high-tech" job supports the creation of as many as five others, including low-skill service sector positions.[178] Thus, in hurting the investors underpinning much of the innovation economy, a higher capital gains tax rate in Massachusetts could result in significantly slower job growth in the long run.

An important factor in the potential impact of the surtax is its treatment of capital gains on par with earned income. The Internal Revenue Service (IRS) essentially treats capital gains as separate from income taxes in that capital gains income cannot push a taxpayer into a higher income bracket on their federal taxes. But Massachusetts' graduated income tax would apply a 4% surtax to all annual income greater than $1 million, including income from capital gains. Unlike capital gains' treatment in the federal tax code, capital gains could push a Massachusetts taxpayer into the higher state tax bracket. For venture capitalists and other investors, this fact is a powerful disincentive to invest in startups or other business activity in Massachusetts.

For a tangible example of how higher tax rates make a place less appealing for investors, see the IRS's 2018 SOI (Statistics of Income) database, which includes federal capital gains income reported by taxpayers with incomes of $1 million or more.[179] In 2018, eight of the nine states with no personal income tax had higher than average capital gains among millionaires (see Figure 2). Notably, none of the states considered to be national centers of finance, insurance, and industry, like New York, New Jersey, California, Massachusetts, and Connecticut, are in the top tier for capital gains averages. Instead, most of the states with the top capital gains averages among the wealthy, including Nevada, Florida, and Wyoming, have no capital gains taxes. Such evidence seems to make a common-sense case for the argument that taxpayers do in fact take state tax rates into consideration when deciding where to take capital gains income.

Raising taxes on capital gains via a graduated income tax could devastate the financial services industry in Boston, which has played a key role in fueling the region's innovation economy, reflected in the numerous tech start-ups in Kendall Square and the Seaport District. Not only does Greater Boston's financial services industry catalyze job creation in other sectors, but it also employed some 147,000 people in 2019, making up 77% of total state financial services employment.[180]

Under a graduated income tax, Massachusetts' top marginal short-term capital gains tax rate would be the highest in the nation, exacerbating a tax and regulatory environment that has already made it hard for day traders and other investors to contribute to Massachusetts' economy. By imposing a 4% surtax on all annual income greater than $1 million, including capital gains, the graduated income tax would penalize capital formation, which is the key to long-term growth and higher living standards for all in the Commonwealth.

But it's not just the financial services industry, and the tech start-ups in which it invests, that will be hurt by such high capital gains tax rates. The profile of the investor most likely impacted by the surtax is more complicated than an advocacy campaign would paint. Because it includes capital gains in its calculations, the surtax would also penalize older homeowners and small business owners who seek to reap in retirement reward for years of investment. These are not fat cats, but folks who have invested years, often decades, of sweat and equity into their establishments and their communities. We look at the impact the surtax will potentially have on these constituents in the remainder of this chapter and the beginning of the next one.

## A Tax on Small Businesses

At a time when many small business owners are still struggling from the economic impacts of COVID-19, it is highly risky to enact a tax on such businesses. Within the broader category of small business owners, pass-through businesses—those structured as partnerships, limited liability companies, sole proprietorships, and subchapter S corporations—are taxed through the owners' individual returns, and thus could be subject to the proposed 4% surtax in Massachusetts. The graduated income tax could become a deterrent to establishing small businesses in the Commonwealth, limiting future growth in the sector, which accounts for a large percentage of private sector activity in the state.[181]

As COVID-19 restrictions subside and profitability returns, these businesses could face a new burden just as they are recovering from the hardships of the pandemic. New taxes could also deter future entrepreneurs from starting businesses here.

### Pass-through Businesses Overview

Although large, publicly traded corporations like Amazon and Microsoft are perhaps the most visible actors in the US private sector, pass-through businesses account for the majority of private sector income and make up 95% of US businesses overall.[182] Pass-through businesses are taxed at the individual level rather than the corporate level, since pass-through business owners elect to have their enterprises' income flow through their individual tax returns. In contrast, C corporations are subject to corporate income taxes and their owners (shareholders) are taxed separately from the entity.[183] Owners of pass-through entities avoid the double taxation that occurs when profits are taxed first on the corporate level and again on the individual level as corporate dividends.[184]

In Massachusetts, 47.8% of employees at private, for-profit sector firms worked for pass-through entities in 2019.[185]

Many attribute the sizable growth of pass-through enterprises to a variety of tax reform measures passed in recent decades.[186] The Tax Reform Act of 1986 made individual tax rates lower than corporate rates, prompting growth in the pass-through business sector. Secondly, the "check-the-box" rule of 1996 allowed businesses themselves to choose whether to be treated as a corporation or a pass-through entity for tax purposes. Prior to the rule change, the IRS determined an entity's tax status via multifactor *Kintner* regulations that enumerated the six characteristics of a corporate venture.[187] These tax and regulatory changes have led to a sizable increase in both the number of pass-through establishments and their share of overall US employment. The Tax

Cuts and Jobs Act of 2017 made such business structures even more attractive by allowing the owners of pass-through entities to deduct up to 20% of net business income on their personal returns.

### Effects of the Graduated Income Tax on Pass-through Businesses in Massachusetts

The surtax proposal would have an adverse effect on owners of pass-through businesses, and particularly on sole proprietors. According to the U.S. Census Bureau, sole proprietorship is the most common form of business ownership in the country, representing 41% of all businesses, with more than 21 million sole proprietors registered in 2015.[188] The Small Business Administration reports that sole proprietors account for 73.2% of U.S. small businesses.[189] The income and capital gains earned by these businesses could become subject to the proposed surtax because it is taxed as pass-through income to the owner.

Figure 3: Number of tax returns declaring income from partnerships or S-corporations in Massachusetts, 2010–2018[190]

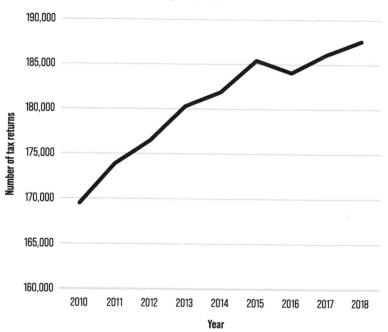

Mirroring national trends, Massachusetts has seen growth among pass-through businesses in recent years (Figure 3). According to IRS tax data, there were 187,580 total partnerships and S corporations in Massachusetts in 2018, a marked increase from 169,490 in 2010. Further, as Figure 4 shows, the share of pass-through entities in the Commonwealth with adjusted gross income above $1 million has also risen in recent years. These are the entities that would be subject to the proposed surtax. Therefore, based on 2018 data, the surtax may apply to as many as 13,430 businesses, or 7.16% of total partnerships and S corporations in Massachusetts, depending on the number of owners to which each entity allocates profit.

**Figure 4: Share of Massachusetts partnership and S-corporation tax returns reporting at least $1 million in income, 2010–2018[191]**

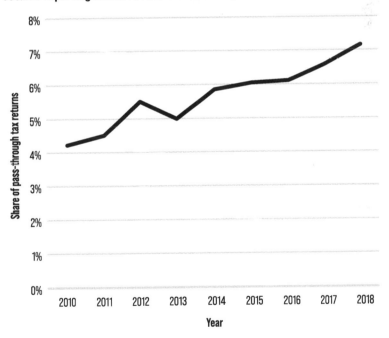

Both overall growth and the growth of high-earning pass-through firms suggest that Massachusetts has had a friendly business climate for smaller proprietors in recent years. But there are no guarantees that the trends exhibited in these graphs will continue if the surtax passes; the academic literature and qualitative evidence from nearby states suggest they won't.

One study of 6,817 tax returns that included schedule C from 1985 and 1988 found that higher income taxes lowered firms' gross receipts.[192] The study chose to assess these years since the Tax Reform bill in 1986 significantly altered the tax environment, and the authors wanted to test whether reducing individual tax rates would prompt greater entrepreneurship. Their results suggest that an individual's decision to enter into a sole proprietorship is a function of the overall individual tax rate. Massachusetts' proposal to implement a surcharge on individual incomes greater than $1 million is particularly concerning for the future of pass-through entities in the Commonwealth because of fears that higher individual rates would correspond with fewer pass-through firms.

A different study, this one of macro-level economic data for European countries, found that, controlling for other variables, there is a negative relationship between average and marginal tax rates and entrepreneurship.[193] Further, the study looked at the relationship between tax progressivity and entrepreneurship by income and found that, for those making significantly above average incomes, greater tax progressivity exhibited a statistically significant negative relationship with entrepreneurship. For individuals who made less than average incomes, there was a positive relationship between tax progressivity and entrepreneurship.

The finding about less entrepreneurship among high-income individuals seems particularly relevant when thinking about the proposed graduated income tax. Given that higher income individuals will be affected by the surtax, it could discourage them from establishing pass-through businesses in the Commonwealth.

In other states that have either enacted income tax hikes or tried to do so, small business groups have been vocal about the negative consequences of the tax increases. In Connecticut, for example, business groups objected to proposals to raise income taxes in 2019. Since the 2019 proposal came on the heels of a 2018 law that altered taxation on pass-through entities, business groups worried that additional changes to pass-through taxation laws would reduce the state's small business hiring rates and overall competitiveness.[194] The executive director of the Connecticut Society of CPAs, Bonnie Stewart, argued that "raising taxes by $50 million and changing a complex policy just one year after adoption could discourage owners from adding jobs, expanding product lines or services, or from purchasing new equipment."[195] Farmington-based CPA Robert Lickwar added that his clients have been vocal in opposing the 2019 bill and that he worried the proposal would deter "new businesses from locating here."[196]

New Jersey business groups also worried about the effects of income tax hikes on pass-through businesses. After many years of trying, the state passed a millionaires tax in September 2020.[197] When the millionaires tax was debated in 2019, prior to its passage, Michele Siekerka, the New Jersey Business and Industry Association's president and CEO, argued that a tax hike on annual income over $1 million would negatively impact "more than 4,000 small businesses whose owners pay taxes on business income through their personal tax returns."[198] A Tax Foundation analysis of New Jersey's recently enacted millionaires tax argues that at a time "when many businesses are struggling to survive and meet payroll, cutting into the profits of businesses that *are* staying afloat is the opposite of an economic recovery strategy."[199] The Tax Foundation already ranks New Jersey as the least competitive state on their State Business Tax Climate Index, and its recent tax increase seems likely to further erode the state's competitiveness.[200]

These anecdotes from Connecticut and New Jersey should concern Massachusetts residents. In 2018, 17,534 Massachusetts taxpayers had both incomes over $1 million and either Schedule C or Schedule E income, which income often comes from pass-through businesses.[201] This is substantive evidence that the proposed surtax could harm some of the Commonwealth's most entrepreneurial and innovative residents.

Finally, among the various pass-through entities that could be affected by the surtax are restaurants and hospitality firms. Pioneer previously explored the acute impact of the COVID-19 pandemic on restaurants, retail, and hospitality firms, and it seems possible that the graduated income tax could pose an additional burden for high grossing firms in these sectors.[202] Although there does not seem to be any data on the precise number of restaurants or hospitality enterprises in Massachusetts that are pass-through businesses with more than $1 million in income, it is reasonable to assume that even these higher grossing entities have struggled during COVID-19. Thus, it would be both risky and unfair to subject these businesses to a new tax once they begin to recover, which would be as late as 2023, precisely when the surtax would kick in.[203]

In sum, the graduated income tax would not only hit Massachusetts' highest-paid corporate executives; it would hit successful independent business owners who elect to form their businesses as pass-through entities. In recent years, the Commonwealth has seen growth in the number of pass-through businesses overall and of those that would be subject to the surtax. But as qualitative anecdotes from Connecticut and New Jersey suggest, if the surtax becomes law, it could impede the future growth of pass-through businesses in Massachusetts.

Finally, at a time when so many small business owners, including those who run pass-through establishments, are hurting from the economic damage wrought by the COVID-19 pandemic, Massachusetts leaders should be as accommodating as possible to smaller proprietors. Policy should strive to accelerate business growth, not to hamper it.

## Punishing Businesses that Reinvest in Growth:

As we note throughout this book, advocates of the proposed 4%

surtax on personal income of $1 million or more argue that it is a way to make Massachusetts millionaires pay their fair share of taxes. But, as we also noted in the previous section, the proposal applies not only to personal income but to profits of partnerships, LLCs, S-Corporations, and sole proprietorships whose income is taxed as "pass-through income" on individual tax returns. Here we explore in greater detail what the potential impact of such an application would mean, reemphasizing that adopting the proposed surtax would impose a major tax increase on Massachusetts businesses at a time when many are struggling to recover from the economic effects of the COVID-19 pandemic.

Under the terms of the proposed constitutional amendment, pass-through income from businesses is included in determining whether a taxpayer is subject to the proposed 80% tax increase (from 5% to 9%) on income of $1 million or more. The applicable language of the proposed constitutional amendment states:

> In addition to the taxes on income otherwise authorized under this Article, there shall be an additional tax of 4 percent on that portion of annual taxable income in excess of $1,000,000 (one million dollars) reported on any return related to those taxes.[204]

Data from the U.S. Census Bureau and the Internal Revenue Service demonstrate that the proposed surtax on the income of pass-through entities would have far-reaching effects. The Census Bureau estimated that Massachusetts had a total of 164,785 private, for-profit business establishments in 2019. Of these, 115,198 (69.9%) were S-corporations, Partnerships, or Sole Proprietorships (so-called pass-through businesses) while just 49,587 (or 30.1%) were C-corporations.[205]

The Census Bureau also estimated that 2,661,056 persons were employed by Massachusetts private, for-profit business establishments in 2019. Of these 1,273,224 (47.8%) were employed by S-corporations, partnerships, or sole proprietorships (so-called pass-through businesses) while 1,387,832 (52.2%) were employed by C-corporations.[206]

Figure 5: Number of Massachusetts Private For-Profit Establishments, By Category (2019)

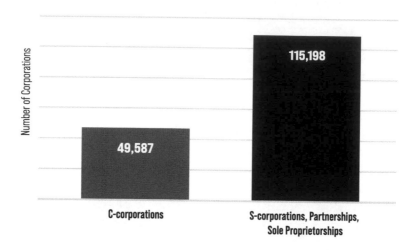

Figure 6: Number of Employees Employed by Massachusetts Private For-Profit Establishments, By Category (2019)

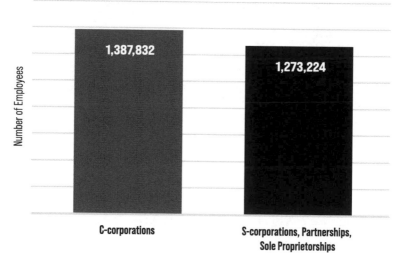

Further, analysis of Internal Revenue Service data from tax year 2018 shows that 33.5% of the income of Massachusetts taxpayers with AGIs of $1 million or more came from partnerships and S corporations.[207]

S corporations are the most common form of business ownership in Massachusetts, representing 45.5% of all for-profit businesses and 65.1% of for-profit pass-through businesses.[208] And S Corporations are already subject to the anti-competitive Massachusetts' "sting tax." Imposing an additional surtax on the income of pass-through entities would only make matters worse for owners of S corporations in Massachusetts.

In a January 21, 2020 article entitled "Reforming Massachusetts Corporate Excise Tax for S Corporations," the Tax Foundation's Michael Lucci described the Massachusetts sting (or "stinger") tax as follows:

"The stinger tax is an extra income tax that is layered on top of the individual income tax and is paid only by S corporation owners. In addition, the competitiveness and economic justification for having a stinger tax should be rethought given how rare it is for a state to impose such a tax.... Massachusetts' corporate code creates an extra tax liability for S corporations that is unique compared to other states. S corporations are pass-through entities for tax purposes, and at the federal level and in the vast majority of states S corp owners are liable only to pay individual income tax on their share of earnings. For Massachusetts taxpayers (and S corp owners), the individual income tax rate is a flat rate of 5 percent. Massachusetts has an additional tax on S corp owners which ranges from 0 percent to 3.9 percent, depending on the industry of the business and its total revenues."[209]

Enactment of the proposed surtax tax would mean that some S corps would be paying 12.9% of their taxable income above $1 million to the state — the 5.0% pass-through personal income tax, the 3.9% sting tax, and the 4% millionaire's tax — while regular C-corporations would still pay an 8% excise tax, although dividends received by C-corporation shareholders would also be subject to tax.

A further adverse effect of the proposed surtax for owners of pass-through businesses is taxation of so-called "phantom income"; i.e. taxable net-income of a pass-through entity that is not distributed to the taxpayer, but is instead reinvested by the company in business operation and business expansion, investments that include infrastructure, capital improvements, purchases of durable equipment, and the hiring of additional personnel. In an article published on July 9, 2018, U.S. News and World Report described phantom income as "income that is attributed to one's tax liability, but without receiving the cash to offset the tax liability."[210]

Under the terms of the proposed constitutional amendment, a partner or member's proportionate share of taxable net income from a pass-through entity is counted in full in determining his or her tax liability, including the tax on income in excess of $1 million that would be subject to the proposed surtax, whether or not the partner or member has actually received the income in the form of distributions.

John Fish, CEO of Suffolk Construction Company, the company that served as general contractor for General Electric's Boston headquarters, the Mullins Memorial Center at UMass-Amherst, and the Encore Boston Harbor casino in Everett, has argued that the "phantom income" problem associated with the proposed surtax will become a drain on the Massachusetts economy.

In an April 2017 *Commonwealth Magazine* article entitled "Millionaire's tax or business tax? Businesses say proposal may hurt growth in Massachusetts," Fish is quoted as saying "you're taking what I would argue is the economic driver of job creation in the commonwealth, and you're penalizing it." Fish then evoked memories of the relatively recent past, saying the surtax is "going to hearken back to days of 'Taxachusetts.'"[211]

Fish explained that 25 to 35% of Suffolk's net income is typically reinvested, rather than being distributed to owners. If the Massachusetts voters pass the so-called "millionaire's tax" next year, he says that while he won't leave the state, he may start looking to take more of his business elsewhere. His return on investment in the Bay State would be hit that hard, Fish believes. "I would deploy capital in other parts of the country," he said.

"We're going to have to have an adult conversation, so to speak. People need to understand the consequences of this, and my concern is the unintended consequences."[212]

Imposing a steep tax increase on businesses incentivizes owners to invest beyond the borders of Massachusetts. For business owners of partnerships, LLCs, S-corporations, and sole proprietorships whose income is taxed as "pass-through income" on individual tax returns, the proposed surtax will only make Massachusetts a less competitive business environment at the worst possible time.

Chapter 4

# A Tax Trap for Businesses, Homeowners and Retirees

### Who Are You Calling a "Millionaire"?

As detailed in Chapter 1, in recent decades, Massachusetts policymakers have worked hard to shed the "Taxachusetts" label that plagued the Commonwealth into the 1990s. Once at 6.25%, the state income tax had fallen to 5% by 2020, while corporate tax rates have been flat.[213] So far in the 21st century, Massachusetts tax policy has prioritized stability and predictability. But since 2015, proponents of the graduated income tax proposal have sought to undermine those priorities under the guise of a "fair" tax only on the super-wealthy.

Despite its purported goal of taxing only the uber-rich, the graduated income tax would fail to protect people of more modest means from overtaxation on one-time incomes. It has the ability to push into higher tax brackets those who, with the sale of a valuable asset, see significant capital gains in one year, punishing owners of retirement nest eggs and desirable real estate. In practice, these "one-time millionaires," who cash in on a lifetime of work and sacrifice in anticipation of retirement, outnumber those who consistently receive seven-figure salaries or stock market windfalls.

Further, as noted in the previous chapter, because of the tax treatment of pass-through business income, many of these "one-time millionaires" could be small business owners still reeling from the economic effects of COVID-19.

It must be stated at the outset of this discussion that Pioneer Institute questions the legality of the view held by amendment proponents and the Massachusetts Department of Revenue that the amendment should be interpreted as applying to income from short and long-term capital gains. Pioneer Institute believes that the proposed amendment is poorly worded and should be revised before any further move toward passage is taken. However, whether ultimately determined to be legal, the inclusion of short- and long-term capital gains under the graduated income tax proposal is a dangerous idea, and we present an analysis in this chapter based on DOR's initial interpretation.

## Who Is a Millionaire?

At the individual level, the graduated income tax casts a wide net. The tax's calculation of income is not limited to salary or wages; it includes one-time income from the sale of a business or home and other forms of capital gains, interest, dividends, partnership distributions, income from pass-through entities, and all other sources of income. The upshot is that, though the proposed surtax would apply to hedge fund managers and technology magnates who earn salaries greater than $1 million annually, it would also constitute a 4% surtax on investors and pass-through businesses with total incomes greater than $1 million.

Under the terms of the proposal, capital gains, which do not affect tax brackets on federal returns, can push a taxpayer into the higher Massachusetts bracket. In the case of the sale of a home or business, the proposal would amount to a substantial tax on retirement.

Many economists agree that higher taxes on capital gains hamper investment, reduce productivity, and ultimately slow down wage growth.[214] As we also noted in the previous chapter, a study by Nobel laureate Robert Lucas estimates that if the U.S. eliminated its capital gains and dividend taxes, the capital stock of American plants and equipment would be 50% larger.[215]

## The Impact on Small and Pass-through Businesses

Capital gains from pass-through businesses far outstrip those associated with the financial services industry. In 2016, the Internal Revenue Service published its most recent comprehensive analysis on the topic, entitled "Sales of Capital Assets

Data Reported on Individual Tax Returns, 2007–2012."[216] The report found that net capital gains from pass-through businesses during this period were by far the largest source of capital gains reported by taxpayers on individual tax returns, totalling $1.25 trillion, which is 49.8% of all capital gains. In comparison, total capital gains from the sale of stocks, mutual funds, and bonds were $511.44 billion, less than half as much, representing 20.3% of all capital gains. In addition, capital gains from the sale of ownership interest in partnerships, S corporations, and estate and trust interests totaled an additional $183.8 billion in capital gains.[217]

These data demonstrate that the proposed graduated income tax, if adopted, would be a tax on businesses, including small pass-through businesses, as they attempt to recover from the COVID-19 recession in many economic sectors (as we discussed in greater detail in the previous chapter). For owners depending on gains from the sale of these businesses as their principal source of retirement funding, the graduated surtax proposal represents a tax on retirement income.

**The Impact on Homeowners**

The proposed surtax also does not include a safeguard to prevent capital gains, after exclusion of $250,000 for single filers or $500,000 for joint filers, on the sale of a principal residence or long-held small business property from pushing a taxpayer into the 9% tax bracket. This is contrary to how taxes are treated at the federal level, where capital gains cannot force a taxpayer into a higher bracket. The graduated income tax will thus ensnare many families that few would consider to be "millionaires," who instead have large amounts of capital gains in a single year due to the sale of a long-owned home or small business.

By including capital gains in the computation of annual income that exceeds the $1 million threshold, the graduated income tax effectively taxes the extraordinary escalation of Massachusetts housing prices that has occurred in recent decades. One example of such growth occurred in the city of Cambridge, where the median price of a single-family home has more than quintupled in 25 years, from $315,000 in May 1996 to $1.66 million in May 2021, while, by comparison, the Consumer Price Index rose by only 67%.[218] Seniors and small business owners who have owned their homes or business property for many years and are relying on decades of appreciation upon retirement will find themselves among those subject to the 4% surcharge, even if their ordinary income otherwise falls well below the million-dollar threshold.

### The Retirement Tax

To understand who exactly would be affected by the so-called "Fair Share" tax proposed by the legislature, it is critical to ascertain how often so-called "millionaires" earn $1 million or more in a year. Fortunately, the Tax Foundation's data on the persistence of millionaires allow us to do just that.

Figure 1: Number of years from 1999 – 2007 in which the period's U.S. millionaires reported making over $1 million[219]

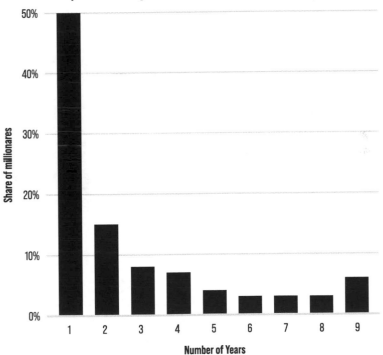

89

According to the Tax Foundation's "Income Mobility and the Persistence of Millionaires, 1999 to 2007," half of U.S. taxpayers who reported gross annual income of $1 million or more at least once over a nine-year period did so only once.[220] Nearly two-thirds did so two or fewer times, and almost three-quarters did so three or fewer times. Fewer than 20% did so in a majority of the nine years and fewer than 6% earned $1 million or more every year (see Figure 1).

**Figure 2: Number of years from 2008 – 2017 in which the period's Massachusetts millionaires reported making over $1 million [221]**

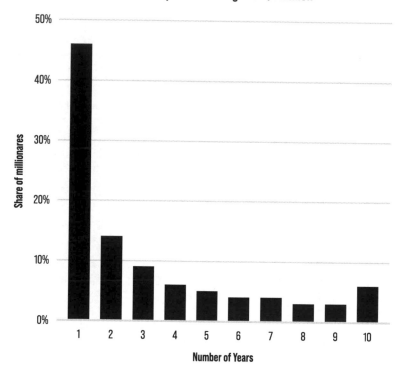

The data expose a vulnerability of the proposed graduated income tax, showing it to be more of a "retirement tax," as many people rely on recouping the value from home equity or a stake in a business to pay for their retirement. Massachusetts displays the very same concentration of "one-time millionaires" as identified nationally by the Tax Foundation. In the Commonwealth,

46% of households reporting incomes greater than $1 million did so only once in 10 years and fully 60% did so twice or less in the 10-year period ended in 2017 (see Figure 2).[222]

These data alone do not prove that many "millionaires" are retirees, or whether those who are using the income to pay for retirement try to avoid taxes on that income. However, information from the IRS shows that after similar graduated income tax levies passed in other states, out-migration exploded among people of retirement age. The so-called "Fair Share" tax would apply to—and dampen the retirement plans of—a significant number of people who worked a lifetime and who are not consistent millionaires.

**Figure 3: Net change in adjusted gross income from people ages 65 and up moving in and out of California and Florida, 2012 – 2018**[223]

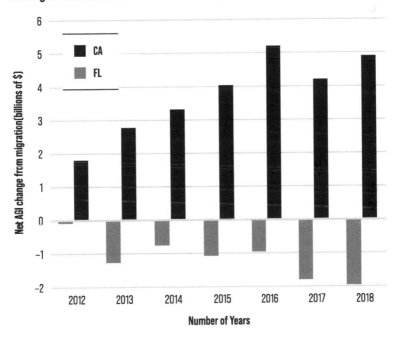

In 2012, the same year California passed Proposition 30, it lost about $87.2 million in adjusted gross (taxable) income (AGI) from people of retirement age moving out of state. The next year, it lost a stunning $1.26 billion on net from these migrating seniors, more than a 14-fold increase compared to the previous year (see Figure 3).[224] In this age category, California maintained 9- and 10-digit AGI losses for every subsequent year on record through 2018. Meanwhile, notable retiree destination (and income-tax-free) Florida gained nearly $1.8 billion from migrating seniors in 2012, and as much as $5.2 billion in subsequent years, in a generally increasing pattern.

The bottom line is that individuals with consistent annual incomes of $1 million or more are not the only ones who will be subject to the "Fair Share" tax. Instead, included in Massachusetts' new top income tax bracket will be many people who wisely invested in a business or real estate at the right time and merely want to remain comfortable in their old age by cashing in on those investments. Thus, the so-called "millionaires tax" is really a retirement tax for many who will be subject to it in a given year, and only in part a tax on the super-wealthy.

Before Massachusetts voters approve this constitutional amendment, the following facts must be considered:

1. The graduated income tax proposal will take a significant bite out of the retirement nest eggs of many small business owners and longtime homeowners.
2. The surtax could hinder economic efforts to recover from COVID-19 by discouraging capital investment and making it harder for business owners to hire back workers.
3. A sizable plurality of Massachusetts million-dollar earners only have a seven-figure annual income once in a 10-year period, an indication that most people affected by the surtax will not be the uber-wealthy technology magnates and hedge fund managers usually associated with the term "millionaire."
4. When California levied a similar tax hike on high earners in 2012, it experienced a 14-fold increase in annual net taxable income losses due to seniors leaving the state, amounting to nearly $1.3 billion in 2013 alone. In 2018, this number had still failed to return to pre-tax hike levels.

Without subjecting the graduated income tax proposal to further scrutiny, Massachusetts voters risk significantly damaging the economy, spurring cycles of capital disinvestment and lower productivity that will reach all corners of the state, and destabilizing the budgets of both the state government and countless senior citizens.

Now, proponents of the surtax argue that the escalation factor built into the proposal will prevent older homeowners getting caught in the retirement trap and insure that only those who can afford it will pay the higher 9% rate. But, as with so much of the rhetoric being used to advocate for the proposed surtax, there is a grave flaw in the proposed escalation factor, which we explore below.

## Bracket Creep Could Make Many More Taxpayers into "Millionaires"

Despite the surtax's potential to harm the broader Massachusetts economy by inhibiting capital formation and innovation, proponents of the graduated income tax proposal advertise that it contains a protection "to ensure that the tax continues to apply only to the highest income residents, who have the ability to pay more." Namely, "the million-dollar threshold would be adjusted each year to reflect cost-of-living increases."[225] The drafters of the new tax propose to accomplish this by including in the state constitution a provision that "this $1,000,000 (one million dollars) income level shall be adjusted annually to reflect any increases in the cost of living by the same method used for federal income tax brackets."[226] Since 2017, this adjustment method has been the Chained Consumer Price Index for All Urban Consumers — U.S. City Average (C-CPI-U) for the 12-month period ending in August of each year. Prior to 2017, the federal government used the Consumer Price Index for All Urban Consumers — U.S. City Average (CPI-U) for this purpose, but switched to the C-CPI-U upon enactment of the Tax Cut and Jobs Act of 2017.

The CPI-U and C-CPI-U track changes in prices of approximately 80,000 goods and services that fall into eight major groups, including food and beverages, housing, apparel, transportation, medical care, recreation, education, communication, and others.[227] While the CPI-U and C-CPI-U are useful for tracking the affordability of these commonly-purchased items and necessities, neither aligns well with the escalation of household income, wages, and salaries in Massachusetts.

It's worth noting that Congress frequently adjusts individual income tax rates and estate tax exemption levels to meet the needs of the times.[228] By contrast, Massachusetts' proposed surtax would lock the C-CPI-U escalation method into the state constitution, making it very difficult to reform as needed. Also, the top federal income tax bracket is far less than $1 million, making price indices a more relevant metric to bracket adjustments.[229] This is because prices of consumer goods are highly relevant to taxpayers in most income brackets, but not as much to high-income taxpayers, who tend to spend a smaller proportion of their income on consumer goods.[230]

Regardless, the main problem with using the C-CPI-U as the escalation index for the constitutional surtax proposal, as proposed by the state legislature, is precisely that it so significantly lags the historical rate of increase of salaries, wages, and household income in Massachusetts. The clearest evidence of this shortcoming is the discrepancy between the Massachusetts legislature's recent pay raises, which are based on aggregate wages and salaries in the state, and what they would have been under a C-CPI-U escalation index (see Figure 4).

Figure 4: Comparison of most recent legislative salary increases in Massachusetts to hypothetical increases under a C-CPI-U escalation factor[231]

|  | Actual increase, based on rise in aggregate wages and salaries in MA | If raise had been based on C-CPI-U |
|---|---|---|
| Base pay increase on Jan 2019 | 5.93% | 3.26% |
| Base pay increase on Jan 2021 | 6.46% | 3.06% |
| Compounded base pay increase | 12.77% | 6.42% |

In 1998, the state legislature proposed (and voters approved) an amendment to the state constitution to increase the base compensation of members of the general court every two years by a defined escalation index. The index that legislators included in the state constitution for this purpose was the change in median household income in Massachusetts for the preceding two year period as reported by the U.S. Census Bureau. This is an appropriate escalation factor for public employee salaries that will ensure raises remain aligned with those of the private sector.

By the same token, using the median household income as an escalation factor for the surtax would ensure that the less well-off are not punished with a higher tax rate for wage gains they reap in the coming years. Instead, the current escalation factor, the C-CPI-U, has historically lagged far behind wage indexes for Massachusetts (see Figures 5 and 6).[232]

**Figure 5. Cumulative percentage increase in CPI-U, C-CPI-U, MA aggregate wages and salaries, and MA median household income (2014–2019)[233]**

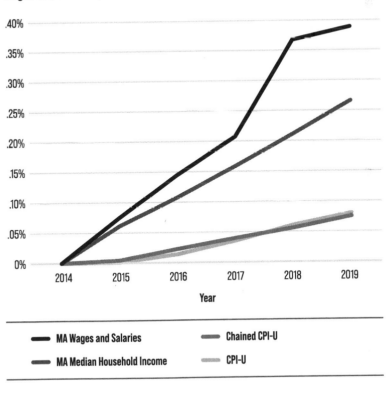

Figure 6. Percentage increase in CPI-U, C-CPI-U, MA aggregate wages and salaries, and MA median household income (1999–2019)[234]

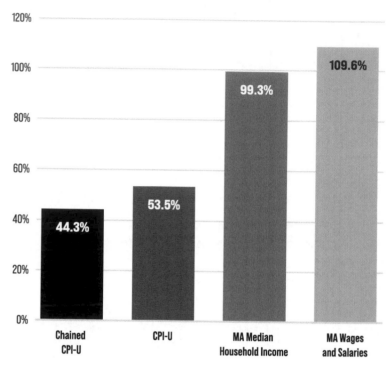

Between 2014 and 2019, Massachusetts median household income increased by 38.9%, a rate more than four times greater than that of the CPI-U and C-CPI-U. Over the same period, Massachusetts aggregate wages and salaries increased by 26.6%, more than three times faster than the CPI-U or C-CPI-U, which increased by 7.5% and 8.0%, respectively.

In the 20-year period from 1999–2019, Massachusetts median household income and aggregate wages and salaries rose more than twice as much as the C-CPI-U. Figure 6 demonstrates that over this 20-year period, the C-CPI-U increased by 44.3% and the CPI-U increased by 53.5%, while median household income in Massachusetts increased by 99.3% and aggregate wages and salaries in Massachusetts increased by 109.6%.

Figure 7. Annual rates of increase (ARI) of CPI-U, C-CPI-U, MA aggregate wages and salaries, and MA median household income in 5-year increments (1999–2019)[235]

| Period | CPI-U | C-CPI-U | MA median household income | MA aggregate wages and salaries |
|---|---|---|---|---|
| 5 years (2014-2019) | 1.55% | 1.45% | 6.79% | 4.83% |
| 10 years (2009-2019) | 1.77% | 1.48% | 3.98% | 4.45% |
| 15 years (2004-2019) | 2.04% | 1.75% | 3.54% | 3.77% |
| 20 years (1999-2019) | 2.16% | 1.85% | 3.51% | 3.77% |

Figure 8. Comparison of total percentage increase in CPI-U, C-CPI-U, and the mean household income received by each fifth and top 5 Percent of all U.S. households over various time periods[236]

| Category | 5 years (2014-2019) | 10 years (2009-2019) | 15 years (2004-2019) | 20 years (1999-2019) | 30 years (1989-2019) |
|---|---|---|---|---|---|
| C-CPI-U | 7.5% | 15.8% | 29.7% | 44.3% | N/A |
| CPI-U | 8.0% | 19.2% | 35.3% | 53.5% | 106.2% |
| Lowest fifth | 30.9% | 32.3% | 49.2% | 54.2% | 118.6% |
| Second fifth | 30.8% | 38.9% | 55.1% | 67.0% | 133.6% |
| Middle fifth | 27.6% | 39.2% | 55.2% | 69.2% | 138.3% |
| Fourth fifth | 26.5% | 41.2% | 58.7% | 75.2% | 154.0% |
| Highest fifth | 31.1% | 48.9% | 68.0% | 88.1% | 197.5% |
| Top 5 percent | 35.7% | 52.7% | 70.9% | 91.9% | 226.5% |

Figure 8 compares the *total percentage increase* in CPI-U, C-CPI-U, and the mean income received by each fifth and the top 5% of all households over various time periods. For the top 5% of U.S. households, which includes those that would be directly impacted by the graduated income tax proposal, mean household income grew at nearly 4.8 times the rate of the C-CPI-U— 35.7% to 7.5% the five-year period from 2014–2019. Over the 30-year period from 1989 to 2019, the mean household income of the top 5% likewise grew 2.1 times faster than did the CPI-U, 226.5% vs. 106.2%. The C-CPI-U was not introduced until 1999.

Figure 9. Annual increase in C-CPI-U, CPI-U, and the mean income received by each fifth and the top 5 percent of all U.S. households over various time periods[237]

| Period | 5 years (2014-2019) | 10 years (2009-2019) | 15 years (2004-2019) | 20 years (1999-2019) | 30 years (1989-2019) |
|---|---|---|---|---|---|
| C-CPI-U | 1.45% | 1.48% | 1.75% | 1.85% | N/A |
| CPI-U | 1.55% | 1.77% | 2.04% | 2.16% | 2.44% |
| Lowest fifth | 5.54% | 2.84% | 2.70% | 2.19% | 2.64% |
| Second fifth | 5.51% | 3.34% | 2.97% | 2.60% | 2.87% |
| Middle fifth | 4.99% | 3.36% | 2.97% | 2.66% | 2.94% |
| Fourth fifth | 4.81% | 3.51% | 3.13% | 2.84% | 3.16% |
| Highest fifth | 5.57% | 4.06% | 3.52% | 3.21% | 3.70% |
| Top 5 percent | 6.30% | 4.33% | 3.64% | 3.31% | 4.02% |

Figure 9 compares the *annual rate of increase* of the CPI-U, C-CPI-U, and the mean income received by each fifth and the top 5% of all households over various time periods. For the top 5% of U.S. households, mean household income grew at 4.3 times the rate of the C-CPI-U — 6.30% to 1.45% — over the five-year period from 2014–2019. Over the 30-year period from 1989 to 2019, the mean household income of the top 5% of income-earners grew 1.6 times faster than the CPI-U, 3.70% vs. 2.44%.

These comparisons demonstrate that the growth of the C-CPI-U and CPI-U do not come remotely close to keeping up with the growth of the mean household income of the top 5%. Thus, the graduated income tax proposal would be impacted by bracket creep and leave households that are not millionaires today vulnerable to over-taxation tomorrow.

As time passes, many taxpayers who currently have annual taxable incomes under $1 million will cross the C-CPI-U adjusted million-dollar threshold and become subject to the graduated surtax if the differential between the rate of increase of the C-CPI-U and that of Massachusetts median household income growth from 2009–2019 continues. Despite the fact that the million-dollar threshold will nominally increase each year by the percentage increase in the C-CPI-U, an increasing number of individuals will become subject to the graduated surtax if existing income growth rates continue.

**Figure 10. Income models and graduated income tax million-dollar threshold, escalated at MA median household income (MHI) and Chained CPI-U (C-CPI-U), 2023–2045[238]**

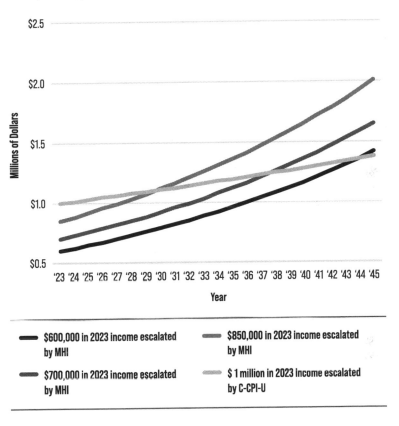

Figure 10 shows that if those rates were to continue into the future, (i.e. with the C-CPI-U increasing by 1.48% annually and the Massachusetts median household income increasing by 3.98% annually) a taxpayer earning $850,000 in 2023 will cross the threshold and become subject to the graduated surtax in the year 2030. A taxpayer earning $700,000 in 2023 would cross the threshold in 2038, and a taxpayer earning $600,000 in 2023 would cross the threshold in 2044.

This phenomenon is modeled in Figure 10 by hypothetical examples of a taxpayer with various annual incomes of less than $1 million in 2023, the first year that the surtax would take effect. He or she would not be subject to the surtax in 2023 because his or her income would be below the $1 million threshold. However, if the filer's taxable income increased over time at a rate higher than the C-CPI-U, eventually he or she could become subject to the graduated surtax. In Figure 6 above, the hypothetical taxpayer's income is projected to increase at the indexed rate of the Massachusetts median household income, 3.98% annually from 2009–2019, while the C-CPI-U rose at the rate of 1.48% annually over the same period.

Because the C-CPI-U is built into the proposed graduated surtax proposal as the escalator, and because the rise in the C-CPI-U has historically failed to keep up with the rise in the Massachusetts median household income, the million dollar threshold will effectively decline over time.

Fairness is at the core of the argument offered by supporters of the graduated surtax proposal. Proponents say the graduated income tax is an effort to force those who have benefited the most from Massachusetts' strong economic growth to pay their "fair share." Just a small subset of the state population—the 20,040, or 0.29%, who earn more than $1 million—would be subject to the tax, supporters insist, leaving the vast majority of Bay State residents untouched.[239] But the new tax proposal, with its inadequate inflation adjustment mechanism, the Chained CPI-U (C-CPI-U), would be anything but fair, especially as time passes.

Supporters of the graduated surtax may argue that it can be modified after passage to alleviate any problems it creates. But if passed by the voters, it would be written into the state constitution, beyond the reach of subsequent legislative amendments. Any changes would require a second constitutional amendment to be passed by both legislative chambers, and then in a statewide popular vote. The best way to spare Massachusetts taxpayers from the adverse consequences of the graduated income tax is to ensure that it never passes in the first place.

We now turn our attention to other flaws in the arguments of the graduated surtax's proponents, beginning with the flawed study proponents use to claim that Massachusetts' taxes are regressive.

# Chapter 5

# Proponents' False Narratives

## Are Massachusetts Taxes Regressive?

Even those who are concerned about the surtax's potential impact on jobs and the economy may share some of the goals of progressive think tanks and advocacy groups in Massachusetts, such as reducing income inequality and advancing "tax fairness." As previously noted, supporters of the proposed Massachusetts graduated state income tax have promoted it as a means of making high income earners pay their "fair share" of state taxes, often taking it as gospel that the current state tax system is regressive.[240]

In a 2015 press release announcing an earlier plan to get the surtax proposal for incomes over $500,000 on the ballot, the SEIU cited a graph purporting that the top 1% of Massachusetts taxpayers pay only 6.4% of their annual income in state and local taxes, while the bottom 20% pay 10.4% (see Figure 1).[241] Their reasoning was as follows:

> "Overall, the Massachusetts tax system is regressive, collecting a larger share of household income from lower-income households than it does from upper-income households... That's why the Raise Up Coalition (strongly supported by all of the SEIU locals in Massachusetts) is planning a campaign to create a tax rate of 9 percent on incomes over $500,000 to raise new revenues that could allow for increased investments in education, child care and transportation."

The graph proponents use to highlight the regressive nature of the current Massachusetts tax code was prepared by the Massachusetts Budget and Policy Center using data from a 2015 Institute on Taxation and Economic Policy (ITEP) report. Multiple organizations, including the Tax Foundation, have raised serious concerns about ITEP's methodology and the sufficiency of its data to demonstrate its conclusions. In a subsequent 2018 tax equality report, even ITEP noted that Massachusetts has a more progressive tax system than most other states. In this chapter, we will explore the validity of ITEP's studies on the regressivity of state tax systems and re-examine the data to highlight the Commonwealth's heavy reliance on a small group of taxpayers to fill state coffers.

**Figure 1: Image from a 2015 Massachusetts Budget and Policy Center report using data from ITEP to purport that Massachusetts tax policies are regressive**[242]

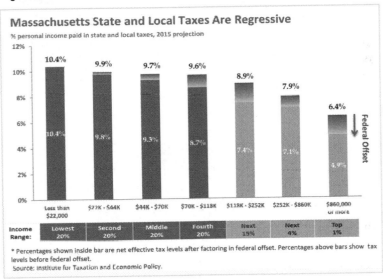

### ITEP's Flawed Study

During the current debate over passing a graduated state income tax, organizations like the Massachusetts Budget and Policy Center, Progressive Massachusetts, and others have made public statements or issued reports using the same data as in Figure 1. The data originate from the 2015 version of a report series published by the Institute on Taxation and Economic Policy (ITEP) called "Who Pays? A Distributional Analysis of the Tax Systems in All 50 States."[243] While ITEP's "Who Pays?" series has been widely cited in the media, many of the assumptions it makes about firms' ability to pass on costs deserve further scrutiny.

ITEP claims that many taxes levied on businesses are ultimately experienced as "indirect taxes" on the end user. ITEP explains that "the inclusion of these passed-through taxes is part of the reason why ITEP's estimates of sales tax incidence can appear to imply that low-income consumers are spending a very large share of their income on taxable items."[244] However, ITEP's methodology lacks transparency about exactly how they calculate this or what portion of the corporate sales tax burden ultimately is borne by consumers under their model. Pioneer Institute reached out to ITEP regarding the details of their tax incidence methodology, but they have failed to respond as of the publication date of this book.

A 1999 study estimated the percentage of the sales tax levy that is ultimately paid by consumers versus that paid by producers. It found an enormous range among states in the share of taxes paid by consumers and producers, depending on the type of goods taxed and how the tax is structured.[245] Overall, the retail sales tax burden on U.S. consumers falls between 28% and 89% of the total tax burden, with the remainder falling mostly on businesses. This variability implies that sales taxes have a relatively progressive effect in some states and a relatively regressive effect in others. In Massachusetts, an estimated 62% of the overall sales tax burden falls on consumers, as opposed to the businesses they patronize. It's unclear from ITEP's publicly available information that they even take state-to-state variations in tax burden into account in their model.

ITEP's calculations also don't count some types of taxes that are fairly progressive. For example, their analysis doesn't treat Massachusetts's estate tax, which for the most part impacts wealthier people, as part of the state tax code, despite the fact that estate tax receipts totaled more than $3.3 billion between fiscal years 2014 and 2020.[246] ITEP also ignores state taxes on health insurance premiums that employers pay for certain insurance arrangements.

## Figure 2: ITEP Tax Inequality Index by state, 2018[247]

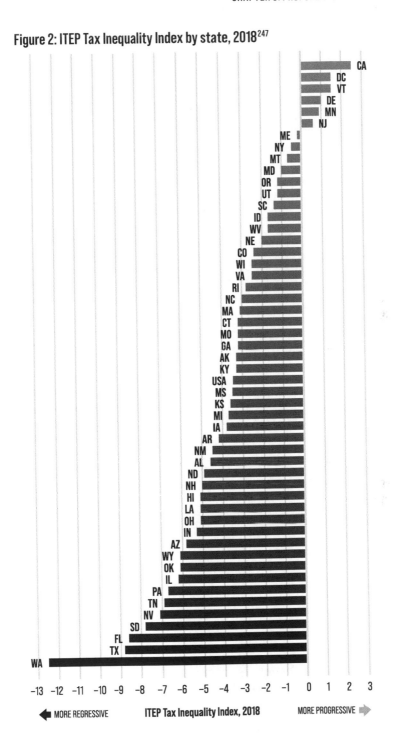

ITEP Tax Inequality Index, 2018

◀ MORE REGRESSIVE     **ITEP Tax Inequality Index, 2018**     MORE PROGRESSIVE ➡

In addition, ITEP ignores how the Massachusetts corporate income tax affects out-of-state actors. Much of the corporate income tax burden ultimately falls on owners and shareholders in other states. This fact contributes to the progressivity of corporate taxes, as local business owners and landlords are likely less well-to-do than large, national corporate executives with tax obligations in several states.[248] However, ITEP excludes the tax burden that falls on out-of-state entities from its analysis, instead focusing only on how state taxes impact Massachusetts-based residents and businesses. If the goal of ITEP's analysis is truly to determine "who pays" for taxes levied by the Commonwealth, as opposed to how much in-state actors pay, this approach is a mistake.

Ironically, ITEP ranks Massachusetts as having a better-than-average Tax Inequality Index score in its most recent "Who Pays?" publication in 2018.[249] It ranked Massachusetts' state and local tax policies as being more progressive than those of 29 other states, scoring the Commonwealth as the 22nd least regressive in the U.S. ITEP cites numerous progressive elements of the Massachusetts tax code, including a refundable earned income tax credit, a sales tax exclusion for groceries, a no-tax threshold and low-income credit that eliminate tax liability for the poorest taxpayers, a combined reporting requirement for the corporate income tax, and a state estate tax. According to ITEP, Massachusetts' Tax Inequality Index score was −3.10, better than the −3.48 average score of the other 49 states and D.C. (see Figure 2).[250]

ITEP also ignores how tax revenue is redistributed after it is collected. Even if the Commonwealth levies a disproportionate amount of taxes on low-income people as a share of their income, its single biggest budget item is Medicaid, which largely benefits lower income populations.[251] Massachusetts spent 29.3% of its fiscal 2020 budget on Medicaid, broadly in line with the national average of 28.6%, and spent a sizable share of the remainder of its revenue on public education (16.1%), which can also reduce income inequality.[252]

Conducting an analysis of who benefits from state spending based on income level would be extremely difficult, but even ITEP is careful to avoid claims that the state tax system as a whole is redistributing wealth from the poor to the rich. Rather, it's plausible that the effect of tax *collection* is slightly regressive, but the effect of state *spending* is strongly progressive, outweighing the regressive elements on the collection side of the equation. A 2019 CBO analysis confirmed that transfer payments tend to reduce market-based inequality at the federal level, but there is scant data to conduct a similar analysis at the state level.[253]

**Figure 3: Amount of Massachusetts income taxes paid by income bracket in 2017, both actual figures and hypothetical if the surtax was in effect[254]**

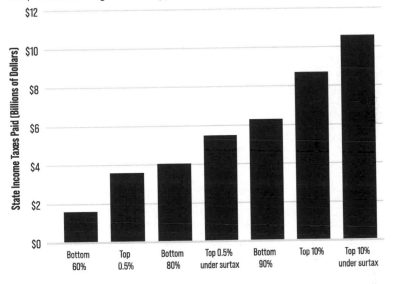

## Considering "Who Pays?" in Absolute Terms

Regardless of ITEP's selective exclusion of certain aspects of the tax code, it's entirely possible that, on the collections side, the tax code is still "regressive" in the sense that higher income people tend to pay a lower share of their income in taxes in a given year. However, the flip side of this is that the wealthy still pay the vast majority of state taxes, especially income taxes.

In 2017, the Massachusetts Department of Revenue (DOR) published a study showing that the 20,159 taxpayers with annual incomes of $1 million or more, constituting 0.5% of state taxpayers, paid $3.60 billion in state income taxes, or 24% of all state income taxes that year. This is 124% higher than the $1.61

billion paid by the bottom 60% of income earners, a total of 2.31 million taxpayers. If the surtax is enacted, tax flight issues aside, the approximately 20,000 taxpayers with incomes of $1 million or more would pay $5.48 billion in state income taxes, which is 32.5% of all state income taxes and 35% more than the bottom 80% of Massachusetts income earners combined.[255] Also in 2017, the top 10% of Massachusetts taxpayers paid 38.2% more than all other taxpayers combined, a figure that would rise to 68.1% more if the surtax passes.[256]

While ITEP's analysis includes more than just income tax data, it is much harder to quantify sales and property tax burdens by income group using existing state-level data in Massachusetts. It is reasonable to assume that the tax incidence of sales and property taxes on lower income populations is relatively greater than on higher income populations. However, according to the Tax Foundation, ITEP's "Who Pays?" series "is overwhelmingly a measure of the progressivity of the individual income tax because, to a significant extent, the rest of the tax code is omitted from ITEP's analysis."[257]

Moreover, by further increasing the share of income tax revenue that comes from such a small sliver of the population, Massachusetts would become more reliant on the wealthy to fill state coffers, while giving those same taxpayers a strong incentive to avoid paying taxes. This paradigm could increase revenue volatility, ultimately making it harder to fund core state programs during times of recession.[258]

### ITEP & The Federal Tax Code

In the past, ITEP's "Who Pays?" analysis watered down the significance of the progressive aspects of the state tax code by including the federal state and local tax (SALT) deduction. This is what the "federal offset" refers to in Figure 1. The SALT deduction effectively reduces what taxpayers pay on their federal returns. It feels distinctly out of place in an analysis of *state and local* tax policy, even if it is calculated based on an individual's state and local tax burden. This has led some of ITEP's critics to accuse them of "cherry-picking one regressive provision in an otherwise highly progressive federal tax code" to "make every state's tax code look significantly more regressive" than it actually is.[259]

Notably, the more recent (2018) version of ITEP's "Who Pays?" analysis doesn't include a "federal offset" visual after the Tax Cuts and Jobs Act of 2017 made the SALT deduction substantially less regressive by capping it at $10,000. In their 2015 analysis, ITEP reported that the richest 1% of Massachusetts taxpayers paid 6.4% of their income in state and local taxes. They then adjusted it down to 4.9% because of the federal SALT deduction.[260] In reality, 6.4% was the more relevant number in 2015, as the "federal offset" reduces what taxpayers pay on their federal returns, not on state returns (see Figure 1). This is one of several ways in which Figure 1 is outdated and misleading.

**Figure 4: Federal and state income taxes paid by Massachusetts tax filers in 2017**[261]

|  | $1M and more AGI | Less than $1M AGI |
|---|---|---|
| Average income - federal (MA returns) | $3,692,966 | $75,924 |
| Average income - state | $3,768,193 | $70,042 |
| Average tax federal (MA returns) | $1,033,763 | $11,339 |
| Average tax - state | $178,481 | $2,979 |
| Average tax - federal & state combined | $1,212,244 | $14,318 |
| Effective tax rate - federal & state combined | 32.8% | 18.9% |

If ITEP had included all the analogous aspects of the federal tax code in their work, their conclusions about the regressivity of the tax code would be very different. The data presented in Figure 4 show the progressivity of the combined federal and state tax system. Taxpayers with adjusted gross income of at least $1 million had an average income of $3.7 million on federal returns and $3.8 million on state returns. They paid an average combined tax of $1,212,244, for an effective tax rate of 32.8%. All other taxpayers had an average income of $75,924 on federal returns and $70,042 on state returns. They paid an average combined tax of $14,318, for an effective tax rate of 18.9%.[262]

Also, in the event that reliance on the wealthy to fill coffers results in higher revenue volatility or slower economic growth, the federal government's ability to borrow money to close budget deficits or finance debt is almost unlimited in the short term, whereas many states, including Massachusetts, have balanced budget requirements. Ultimately, the desire for greater progressivity in state and local tax systems needs to be balanced with sound principles of economics, budget management, and general governance.

To sum up, advocates of the proposed surtax paint a picture of the Massachusetts tax system as highly regressive. They fail to mention that ITEP, the organization that produced the data upon which they rely, rated Massachusetts as having a more progressive tax system than 29 other states. ITEP fails to adequately explain their model's treatment of the tax incidence of sales, excise, and property taxes, and they exclude a number of other aspects of the tax code that make it seem artificially regressive.

Taxpayers with annual incomes of more than $1 million, constituting 0.5% of all taxpayers, paid more than twice as much in state income taxes in 2017 as did the bottom 60% of income earners combined. That same year, the top 10% of Massachusetts taxpayers paid 38.2% more than all other taxpayers combined, a figure that would rise to 68.1% more if the surtax passes.[263] Taxpayers with incomes of $1 million or more had average incomes of $3.7 million in 2017 and paid an average of $1.2 million in combined state and federal taxes, for an effective rate of 32.8%. Other taxpayers had an average income of $70,042 and paid an average of $14,318 in combined state and federal taxes, for an effective rate of 18.9%.[264]

In an era of stark income inequality, the federal government is better able to address progressivity in taxation and the resulting economic fallout. After all, to avoid taxation, it is far more difficult to leave the country than move across state lines. Increasing the top income tax rate in Massachusetts from 5% to 9%, an 80% increase, runs the risk of incentivizing high income taxpayers and businesses to relocate to lower tax states. If the Commonwealth is to have a serious debate about the merits of a tax hike, we should start with a candid look at how progressive our tax code already is, and ITEP's "Who Pays?" series is far from candid.

But the ITEP series is not the only flawed study proponents rely on to advocate for the graduated income tax proposal. They also claim that the prospect of wealth migrating from Massachusetts to other states in the face of such a large tax increase is just rhetoric in the wind. The study they use to dismiss such a prospect, however, is, like the ITEP series on "Who pays?", significantly flawed, as we see in the next chapter.

## Drastically Undercounting Households and Businesses Affected by Their Tax

Surtax advocates argue that similar taxes in other states have had little impact on the migration of millionaires.[265] In support of their argument, they cite Cornell University Associate Professor Cristobal Young, whose research suggests that "millionaires taxes" similar to the one being proposed in Massachusetts have had little impact on millionaire mobility when enacted in other states.

### A Narrow Definition: Counting Only Consistent Million-dollar Earners

Though we welcome Professor Young's work to this debate, he drastically undercounts the number of people who will at some point in their lives be subject to a so-called millionaires tax. Hence, Professor Young and the public policy analyses that cite his work dramatically underestimate the potential for tax flight.[266]

Professor Young does not count taxpayers as being millionaire migrants unless they had filed a federal tax return with adjusted gross income (AGI) of $1 million or more *in the year before they moved.* In a 2016 research paper, Professor Young and his co-authors define millionaire migrants as "people who earned $1 million or more in year t, and changed their state of residency between years t and t + 1."[267] Such a narrow definition of a "millionaire migrant" ignores the possibility that savvy taxpayers changed their domicile to a lower tax state in anticipation of a million-dollar gain from the one-time sale of a valuable asset, thus avoiding the high rates associated with places like New York and California.

To grasp the significance of Professor Young's definitional limitation, consider that it excludes 14.3 million households in the U.S. that had a net worth of $1 million or more but incomes of less than $1 million, according to Federal Reserve Board estimates (see Figure 5).[268] Many of the households portrayed in Figure 5 would be subject to the surtax upon the sale of a portion of their assets, but Cristobal Young's methodology is inadequate to assess the extent to which they engage in tax avoidance.[269]

**Figure 5: Number of U.S. households by category of wealth (2019)[270]**

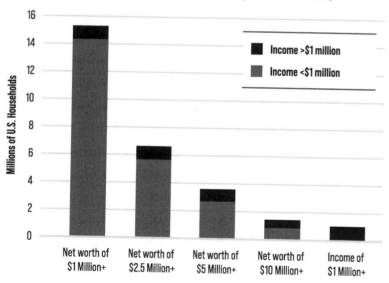

Young's methodology also ignores the fact that the majority of U.S. households with high net worth, defined as greater than $10 million, earn less than $1 million annually. Among this excluded group are more than 850,000 households. (see Figure 6). In fact, 58.9% of households with greater than $10 million in net worth had annual incomes of less than $1 million.[271] Cumulatively, these households have trillions of dollars in unrealized capital gains that may be subject to the graduated income tax upon sale.[272] Future studies of whether millionaire migration is occurring should aim to determine whether graduated income taxes influence the behavior of high-net-worth individuals who happen to make less than $1 million in income most years. More insidiously, a tax like the so-called Fair Share Amendment would also deter high-net-worth individuals from moving to Massachusetts in the first place.

**Figure 6: Share of high-net-worth U.S. households that were million-dollar earners (2019)[273]**

| | Household Income | Net worth of >$1M | Net worth of >$2.5M | Net worth of >$5M | Net worth of >$10M | Net worth of >$100M |
|---|---|---|---|---|---|---|
| Number (& percentage) of Households | <$1M | 14,314,529 (-93.6%) | 5,642,446 (-85.2%) | 2,687,978 (-74.8%) | 857,220 (-58.9%) | 2,645 (-7.7%) |
| | >$1M | 983,540 (-6.4%) | 980,617 (-14.8%) | 904,075 (-25.2%) | 599,115 (-41.1%) | 31,862 (-92.3%) |
| | Total | 15,298,069 (-100%) | 6,623,063 (-100%) | 3,592,054 (-100%) | 1,456,335 (-100%) | 34,507 (-100%) |

While data on the migration patterns of high-net-worth individuals are scarce, the sheer number of people who could potentially be millionaires in a given year by selling a portion of their assets constitutes a vulnerability to tax avoidance. Thus, net worth is a better measure of wealth than prior year income when analyzing migration in response to taxation.

Another way of making this point is to look at data regarding individuals who earn just under $1 million annually. Data from the Federal Reserve Board's 2019 Survey of Consumer Finances, which the American Statistical Association regards as "the most comprehensive [wealth] data available for the United States," show that nearly 1.6 million U.S. households had incomes between $500,000 and $999,999.[274] Of these, the mean net worth is $8.3 million (see Figure 7). While these households would not be subject to the proposed surtax immediately, they may be susceptible to it in the future upon disposition of assets. Also susceptible to future imposition of the proposed surtax are the nearly 5.4 million households with incomes between $250,000 and $499,999, which have a mean net worth of $3.1 million (see Figure 8).

Figure 7. Components of net worth among wealthy U.S. households with incomes <$1 million[275]

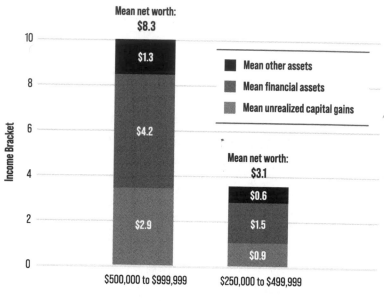

Net Worth (millions of $)

Figure 8: Mean income and components of net worth among U.S. households with incomes from $250,000 – $1 million (2019)[276]

| Household income range | Mean income | Mean unrealized capital gains | Mean financial assets | Mean net worth |
|---|---|---|---|---|
| $250,000 – $499,999 | $340,535 | $927,381 | $1,517,720 | $3,051,673 |
| $500,000 – $749,999 | $608,147 | $2,541,608 | $3,821,872 | $7,487,182 |
| $750,000 – $999,999 | $865,839 | $3,535,194 | $4,959,434 | $10,139,309 |
| $250,000 – $999,999 | $420,072 | $1,366,356 | $2,123,898 | $4,252,196 |

## The Florida Effect

Perhaps the biggest caveat to Young's research concerns Florida, a state that has no income tax, capital gains tax, dividends and interest tax, or estate tax, and is by far the leading destination for U.S. millionaires. He writes that "evidence for tax migration is largely driven by Florida as an attractive destination for U.S. millionaires" and that "[t]he uniqueness of the Florida effect is a very robust finding."[277]

**Figure 9: Net out-migration of taxable income from Massachusetts among destination states with over $500 million in total gains (1993-2018)[278]**

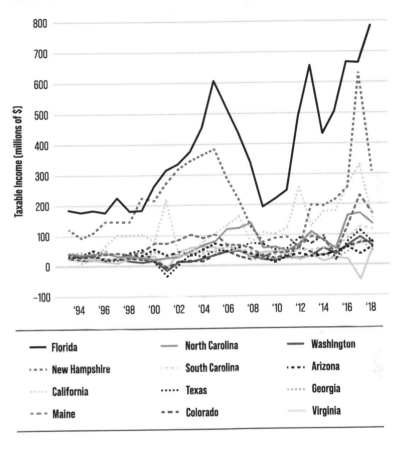

Indeed, Florida accounts for nearly half of Massachusetts' out-migration of adjusted gross income (AGI), far more even than neighboring New Hampshire, another no-income-tax state (see Figure 9). Yet in "Millionaire Migration and Taxation of the Elite," Young and his co-authors conclude that "when Florida is excluded there is virtually no tax migration; when any other state is excluded, our core finding of tax-induced migration is supported."[279] This is akin to saying that if you exclude Muhammad Ali, Louisville hasn't produced any great boxers.

### Do The Wealthy Migrate Away From High-Tax States? A Comparison of Adjusted Gross Income Changes in Massachusetts and Florida

Wealth migration is the entrance and exit of taxable income between states. Beginning with 2011–12 data, the Internal Revenue Service's Statistics of Income Division (SOI) has produced tabulations that show aggregate migration flows by amount of adjusted gross income (AGI) and age of the primary taxpayer.[280] This database allows us to take an in-depth look at current trends in wealth migration and the potential consequences of progressive taxation.

Figure 9 presents IRS data showing Massachusetts' net migration of AGI from 1993 to 2018 for all tax returns regardless of income level. It shows that Massachusetts experienced a cumulative net outflow of more than $20.7 billion in AGI over this period to other states and nations. Earned income tax-free Florida and New Hampshire were the biggest beneficiaries; together they accounted for 72.6% of Massachusetts' net out-migration of AGI over this period. Massachusetts had a net out-migration of AGI to Florida alone of $9.6 billion, representing 46.5% of Massachusetts' total net out-migration.

This trend is largely driven by the disproportionate wealth of those who move from Massachusetts to Florida. The average AGI of such a migrant was $120,325 in 2018, compared with the average AGI of $64,992 among taxpayers who moved from Florida to Massachusetts that year. While migrants to New Hampshire tend to be less wealthy than those that flee to Florida, the Granite State's cumulative AGI gains from Massachusetts over the period still total $5.4 billion, or 26.1% of Massachusetts' total net out-migration. Other states and nations accounted for the remaining $5.7 billion, representing 27.4% of Massachusetts' total net AGI out-migration over this period.[281]

Massachusetts's pattern of net out-migration to Florida and New Hampshire was consistent across 26 years of data. Figure

10 shows which states had the most significant net positive or net negative AGI migration from 1993 to 2018 for taxpayers of all incomes. Notably, if net AGI out-migration to Florida, California, North Carolina, and northern New England were all $0, AGI migration to Massachusetts during this timeframe would be positive overall.[282] This is because Massachusetts was seeing positive net AGI in-migration from other northeastern states like New York, Connecticut, and New Jersey, with smaller positive numbers from much of the Midwest.

**Figure 10. Massachusetts cumulative net AGI inflow/outflow by source & destination, 1993–2018[283]**

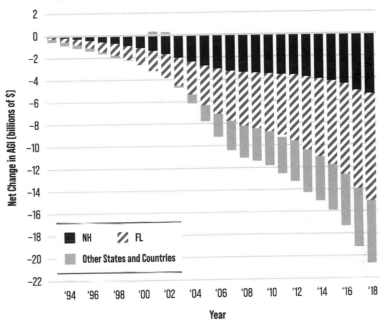

### The Florida Welcome Mat: Sun and Savings

Florida has recently been one of the most attractive destinations for migrating U.S. taxpayers; conversely, only four states (Nevada, North Carolina, Tennessee, and Utah) gained taxable income on net due to wealth migrants moving out of Florida in 2018. The Sunshine State added $182.8 billion in cumulative net AGI from 1993 to 2018 across all income levels, according to IRS SOI data.[284]

As noted, the IRS' 2012 addition of income categories to its income migration data reporting allows researchers to calculate the percentage of AGI income migration attributable to high-income taxpayers by state. The highest income category reported in IRS migration data is annual AGI of more than $200,000. According to IRS data, Florida had a total of 122,341 migration inflow returns of taxpayers with annual AGIs of $200,000 or more from 2012 to 2018. The average AGI of these inflow returns was $777,348, and the value of this income bracket's returns totaled $95.1 billion.[285]

Over the same period, Florida had 53,248 outflow returns of taxpayers with AGIs of $200,000 or more, with an average AGI of $610,385, 21% lower than the average AGI of high-income taxpayers moving into the state. Florida's net AGI attributable to migration from 2012 to 2018 across all income brackets was $88.9 billion, of which 70.4% came from taxpayers with AGI of $200,000 or more (see Figure 11). This massive net AGI migration in just seven years came despite the fact that they constituted only 4.5% of total inflow returns over that period.

Some academics have assured voters that adoption of a surtax would spur minimal migration, citing Cristobal Young's finding that "only" 2.4% of millionaires move each year.[286] But migration patterns create large shifts in wealth between states over time, and the relationship between Massachusetts and Florida exemplifies the scale of this cumulative effect. More than 30% of the total growth in AGI among all Florida taxpayers from 1993 to 2018 was attributable to the state's net increase in migration. Compare that to Massachusetts, and its net outflow of $20.7 billion in AGI over the same period.

Analysts of millionaire migration shouldn't immediately write off Florida as a rare outlier, but rather should explore the likelihood that Florida's friendly tax environment, combined with favorable weather and other factors, make it a uniquely attractive destination for the wealthy. They should also seek to isolate the influence of the tax environment on wealth migration by comparing Florida with states with similar coastal amenities, like South Carolina and California.

## Figure 11. Massachusetts cumulative net AGI migration inflow by source/ destination state, 1993–2018[287]

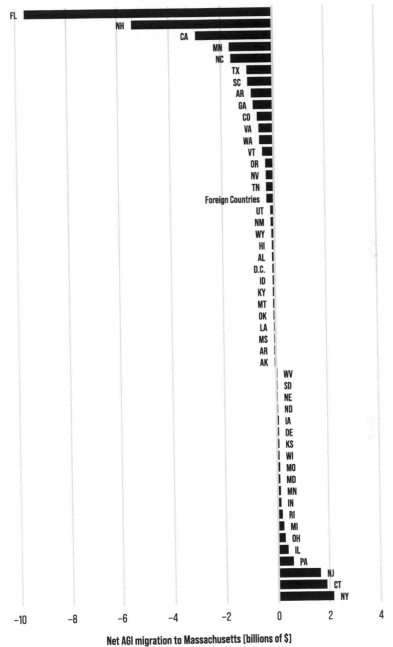

Net AGI migration to Massachusetts (billions of $)

## Figure 12. Share of net AGI in-migration by income bracket in Massachusetts and Florida, 2012–2018[288]

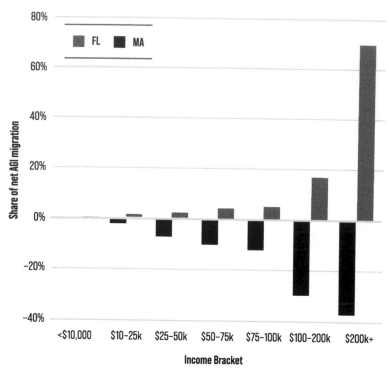

Moreover, other academic research shows that taxpayers, especially the wealthy, do in fact exhibit a significant degree of behavioral responses—such as shifting income to non-taxable sources or changing location—to increases in tax rates. A 2004 paper by National Bureau of Economic Rsearch economists Joel Slemrod and Jon Bakija found that, for every percentage point increase in state personal income tax rates, residents filed 1.5% fewer federal estate tax returns in the state.[289] Another estimated that, when New York cut the average tax rate for the top 1% of earners from 7.5% to 6.85% in 2006, it resulted in a net increase of 28 star scientists to the Empire State.[290] In 2011, the New Jersey Department of the Treasury found that the Garden State's 2004 millionaires' tax drove some 20,000 taxpayers to leave by 2009, taking $2.5 billion in taxable income with them.[291] Saez,

Figure 14. Florida cumulative net annual AGI inflow/outflow by source, 1993 to 2018[296]

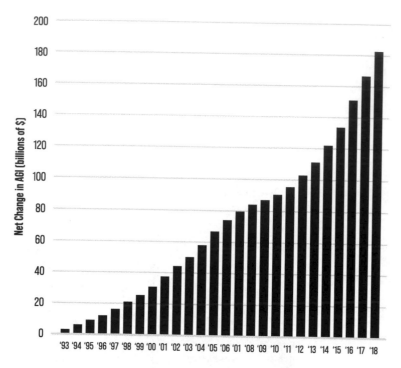

Affluent taxpayers are responsible for an outsized proportion of state tax revenue—no matter the state. The data show a strong correlation between state tax rates and migration. We live in a world where technology allows individuals to be more mobile than ever, and that is especially true for those on the higher rungs of the socio-economic ladder.

A change in the state constitution to create a graduated income tax was approved at a Constitutional Convention vote in June 2021, and will go before state voters in November 2022. As Massachusetts voters consider this proposal to increase income taxes, they must balance any short-term benefit it might bring against the long-term impact it will have on jobs and the economy.

To that end, the following findings must be considered:

1. When the Massachusetts Department of Revenue issued its estimate of how much the surtax would generate, it provided a static analysis. That is why it added an important caveat: "taxpayers may respond to the additional tax by changing decisions on migration, consumption, investment, business location, etc. The number of high-income earners and amount of income reported by those earners could also fluctuate considerably from year to year."[297]

2. Professor Young's definition of "millionaire" is too narrow. By ignoring households with substantial net worth but lower annual incomes, he counts only high earners who consistently earn more than $1 million per year as tax-induced migrants.

3. Young himself cites Florida migration as the big exception to his thesis that wealthy individuals rarely move because of increases in taxes. Massachusetts has experienced high net out-migration of taxpayers ($20.7 billion in adjusted gross income) over the past 23 years. About three-quarters have moved to tax-free New Hampshire and especially Florida. The lure of tax-free states will be even greater because of the rise in remote work after the COVID-19 pandemic.[298]

4. The adoption of a surtax could spur substantial wealth migration. Already Professor Young finds that 2.4% of millionaires move each year.[299] The cumulative effect of an annual loss of high net worth taxpayers of that size can add up to big numbers, and exacerbate the already considerable exodus of Massachusetts residents to Florida.

Voters should think twice before effectively doubling the state taxes of high-income Massachusetts taxpayers and entrepreneurs. This is especially true if remote work remains a reality in our post-COVID world. If our most productive and highest-earning workers can live and work anywhere, as is increasingly possible, why would they choose to live somewhere that seems to treat them only as a piggy bank?

Chapter 6

# Taking Off: Wealth and Business Flight in a Post-COVID World

## Remote Work After COVID-19 Will Accelerate Wealth Flight

Another flaw with relying on pre-COVID studies on millionaire migration to downplay the potential effect of a tax hike is that they do not take into account the rapid proliferation of telecommuting during the pandemic. Global Workplace Analytics, a consulting company based in San Diego, garnered headlines when it predicted that "25–30% of the workforce will be working-from-home multiple days a week by the end of 2021," compared to just 3.6% before the pandemic.[300] Indeed, a September 2021 Gallup poll found that 25% of American employees work remotely full-time, with an additional 20% working remotely at least some of the time.[301] A permanent shift in the popularity of remote work would have major implications for everything from traffic congestion and carbon emissions to commercial real estate.

The geographic implications of such a shift could also be massive as the increased adoption of remote work lowers "barriers to exit" for companies and people once based in and around sprawling metropolises. In November 2020, Forbes Magazine columnist Gad Levanon predicted that the "big winners" of remote work, in terms of attracting residents, would be vacation spots.[302] A shift toward remote work could also accelerate pre-existing migration trends towards southern and western states.

In a damning December 2020 interview with the Silicon Valley Business Journal, artificial intelligence software mogul Tom Siebel said that "every responsible chief executive officer has to consider moving their company out of California."[303] According to Census Bureau estimates, California recorded a population loss for the first time on record between July 2019 and July 2020, and now companies like Hewlett Packard Enterprises and Oracle are following workers out of the state.[304]

Given recent technological innovations, notably teleconferencing apps like Zoom, remote work is only becoming more sophisticated and convenient. Meanwhile, tools like Zoom, G Suite, and Slack make it easier than ever for coworkers to meet and share files and messages over the internet.[305] Technology, combined with shifting attitudes among workers and employers alike, could spell trouble for previous job growth hotspots.

In many ways, individual events in the business world during the pandemic justify such concerns. For example, Goldman Sachs' Asset Management division is mulling a move from Wall Street to Miami, one of many recent examples of businesses rethinking the benefits of being in high-cost cities during the pandemic.[306] Similarly, Palantir Technologies has already moved from Silicon Valley to Denver, and other Silicon Valley firms, notably Facebook, have prepared to permanently offer remote work to more employees after the pandemic. Such moves have reduced the need for employees to be able to afford a coastal California lifestyle (and for firms to pay their workers coastal California wages).[307] A May 2021 survey even found that 36% of Massachusetts businesses planned on reducing their office space footprint in Massachusetts.[308]

## Individual Workers React to the Pandemic

Similar trends are also evident for individual workers. Before the pandemic, economic growth was increasingly concentrated in a small handful of powerful, expensive cities, and access to the innovation economy and labor market often kept workers from moving to cheaper, roomier locales.[309] But after the pandemic hit places like New York City especially hard, stories abounded of wealthy residents decamping to vacation homes in Vermont, Florida, or the Hamptons. It's an open question whether such people will need policy-driven incentives to move back, especially given New York's heavy reliance on the wealthy to fill city coffers. In the words of urban theorist Richard Florida, "it doesn't take very many one-percenters changing their address to wreak havoc on cities' finances."

Figure 1: Share of workers who telecommute before, during, and after the COVID-19 pandemic, according to various survey groups*[310]

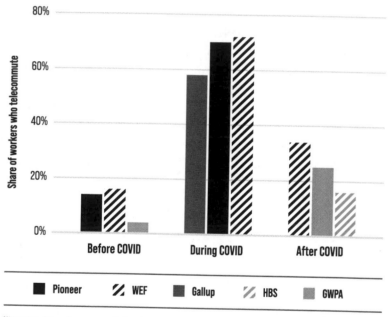

*Note: some of these figures may not be directly comparable to each other, as they poll different groups of people at different times with differently worded questions

The rise of remote work may be the final push for workers and employers already fed up with the enormous costs of living and doing business that plague many coastal metropolises. The pandemic and its repercussions have made it easier for workers of many stripes to live hundreds of miles from their office, and recent research makes the scale of this shift towards telecommuting even clearer.[311]

While 51% of the American workforce worked remotely as of April 2021,[312] as many as 22% of workers are projected to remain telecommuters by 2025, according to an Upwork survey.[313] Harvard Business School offered a lower estimate of 16% of workers telecommuting after COVID-19 subsides, but that's still far more than the 3.6% who worked from home at least half-time before the pandemic (see Figure 1).[314]

Moreover, these remote workers might not be as concentrated in certain companies as one might expect. Before COVID-19, 5% of companies said that at least 40% of their employees were primarily working remotely. One year after the pandemic ends, 34% expect that at least 40% of their employees will be working remotely.[315] Nearly three-quarters (74%) of companies plan on moving at least 5% of their employees to full-time remote work after COVID-19, and nearly a quarter said they would move at least 20% of their employees to remote work.[316]

The work-from-home revolution also reflects shifting attitudes of workers, not just business leaders. In a 2019 survey, 56% of respondents said it's possible to work from home in their line of work, and 80% said they would like to telecommute at least some of the time.[317] Further, 35% of workers said they would change jobs for the opportunity to work remotely full-time, including nearly half (47%) of Millennials.[318] More than one-third of workers even said they would take a 5% pay cut for the opportunity to work remotely at least some of the time.[319] More recently, after the pandemic began, Pioneer Institute found that 56% of workers surveyed would like to telecommute at least two days per week.[320]

### Worker Productivity From Home is High

A growing body of evidence also suggests that there are concrete gains to worker productivity from remote work. A recent survey of tech executives found that 48.6% said that remote work during the pandemic has increased productivity, compared to 28.7% who said remote work has decreased productivity.[321] While information technology might be among the most easily adaptable to remote work, other categories, such as Administrative Support and Real Estate, reported nearly 40% productivity gains from telecommuting as well.[322]

These increased productivity gains have also been observed in rigorous academic studies, not just polls with supervisors. According to an April 2021 working paper out of the University of Chicago, the post-pandemic economy will have a 4.8% productivity premium relative to the pre-pandemic economy, largely because of reduced commute times enabled by remote work.[323] Other researchers claim that for every half-time remote worker, the average employer saves $11,000, largely due to productivity gains and real estate cost savings, while the average telecommuter saves up to $4,000 in travel, parking, and food expenses.[324]

Ultimately, these numbers show the strong incentives both workers and employers have to pursue more telecommuting opportunities in the future. But as the previously high-opportunity places that many choose to leave behind (think New York City or Silicon Valley) see their tax revenues dip, these economic hubs may face a reckoning over how to balance budgets or maintain core services for those who have nowhere else to go. Richard Florida even alludes to the potential for a repeat of the blight and disinvestment that characterized much of New York City during the 1970s.[325]

For some observers, however, the fact that the enormous importance of coastal enclaves for big business over the last generation is waning may be an opportunity to return places like New York and San Francisco to their roots, with small, local businesses, more affordable urban amenities, and lower tax and regulatory burdens.[326] It's also likely that big business operations will remain centered in these and similar cities, even while the individuals who run them reside elsewhere.[327]

New York and California were already known for shedding residents and corporations to more business-friendly locales before COVID-19, but the pandemic has since heightened the need for cautions around policies that might further lower barriers to exit. Inevitably, this means thinking deeply about the incentives and tradeoffs embedded in local, state, and federal policies for years to come.

In addition to policies enacted in expensive coastal states that tend to render them less competitive as places to work and do business, many cities and states are increasingly instituting incentives to attract talented workers and the companies that employ them to middle America. We explore these trends in the next section.

## States and Cities are Creating Incentives to Attract the New Telecommuters

Not only are many Massachusetts taxpayers struggling to emerge from a devastating pandemic-induced recession, but that recession has also given other states and localities more reasons to try to lure away jobs and residents from booming coastal metropolises. Many Commonwealth residents have a newfound ability to telecommute into their workplace from just about anywhere. With historically low mortgage rates and savvy government programs aimed at attracting new residents to once-neglected corners of the country with offers of free real estate and other generous subsidies and benefits, reasons abound for leaving expensive job centers.[328]

The heightened prevalence of tax and regulatory competition among states could exacerbate the economic impact of an unfriendly business environment. At the crux of the issue is the concern that, if employers leave the state, it will be easier than ever for workers to do the same, potentially leading to long-term fiscal and economic problems in the Commonwealth. As Pioneer has argued before, state lawmakers should be especially cautious going forward about policies that would further lower "barriers to exit" for households and firms alike.[329]

### The (Tax) Competition Heats Up

In recent years, there have been numerous high-profile examples of governments using considerable tax breaks and other benefits to lure major corporations across state and even national lines. To cite a couple of examples, the 2018–2019 sweepstakes to determine the home of Amazon's second headquarters and Wisconsin's grant of $4.1 billion in incentives for Foxconn come to mind. A 2020 Princeton study found that, to lure companies,

U.S. state and local governments use tax incentives worth at least $30 billion annually.[330]

Figure 2: Combined value of state and local tax incentive packages for select Amazon HQ2 location proposals[331]

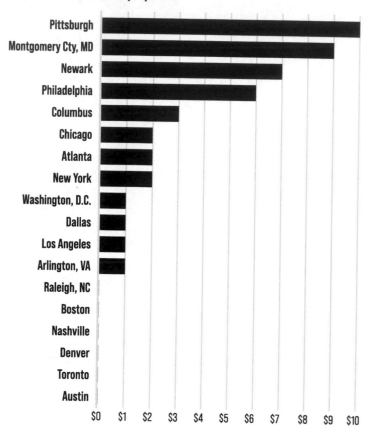

Even places with strong business environments want to attract more economic activity, and tax incentives are seen as a way of getting a leg up on other places with desirable qualities for employers. This logic helps explain why, perhaps contrary to intuition, many large coastal cities with booming economies offered Amazon *more* in tax breaks than many smaller middle-American cities during its second headquarters sweepstakes (see Figure 2). A Brookings Institution postmortem on the Amazon sweepstakes even argued that the amounts of the tax breaks were "largely based on a region's ability to offer incentives," as opposed to the amount needed to attract Amazon to the location.

Regardless of the case-specific justifications cities and states make for competing with each other, the overarching reason is clear: in an increasingly globalized world, both capital and people are highly mobile. A 2018 Urban Institute analysis shows that the three-year migration rate among large firms in particular has almost doubled, from 3% to nearly 6%, between the late 1990s and early 2010s.[332] While the analysis only included select metropolitan areas in the U.S., it also predates the COVID-19 pandemic, which has been a notable catalyst for business relocation.[333]

In recent years, corporate tax competition has taken on an international scope. Examples abound of corporate inversion, in which companies use a merger with a foreign business to change their tax residence to a lower-tax country like Ireland or Switzerland. While this method of tax avoidance was relatively uncommon before the 1990s, many high-profile American companies have performed inversions since 2013, including AbbVie, Medtronic, Chiquita, Pfizer, Apple, Burger King, and Coca-Cola.[334] In addition, as of 2013, Pfizer, one of the largest pharmaceutical companies in the U.S., operates at least 128 foreign subsidiaries in tax havens.[335]

The increasing magnitude of international tax competition even prompted Treasury Secretary Janet Yellen, in April 2021, to propose a "global minimum corporate tax rate," to be enforced by the OECD.[336] Six months later, in October 2021, world leaders at the Rome G20 summit formally agreed to a global minimum corporate tax rate of 15%.[337]

Many public agencies now also pay individual households to relocate, not just firms. As remote work's rising popularity makes it easier for telecommuters to live anywhere, areas that previously struggled to attract new residents have resorted to subsidizing moving costs. Tulsa, Oklahoma; Chattanooga, Tennessee; Baltimore, Maryland; and the entire state of Vermont are prime examples.[338] All of these programs, including Vermont's subsidies specifically for new residents who work remotely, predate the pandemic, and a central selling point of many of them is a lower cost of living than exists in much of urban America.[339]

Of the 37 cities currently paying residents to move there, 28 have median housing prices less than half that of Massachusetts, according to MakeMyMove.com.[340] Massachusetts had the fourth highest home prices in the country in 2021, after California, Hawaii, and Washington State, and Zillow estimates that home prices in the Commonwealth grew by 18.0% during the year ended September 2021.[341] Massachusetts is also one of the most expensive states for childcare, which is important considering the widespread school closures during the pandemic. Overall, reasons abound why individual households would find it especially appealing to move away from Massachusetts in the near future, even as the pandemic subsides.

Many government programs aimed at attracting new residents seem to be working. In 2019 alone, at least 290 people took advantage of Vermont's subsidy plan, which awards up to $10,000 to new residents who work remotely from the state.[342] That's a sizable share of Vermont's overall population change for the year, which the U.S. Census Bureau estimates at a loss of 699 residents between July 2019 and July 2020.[343] While these figures can't definitively prove that the new residents wouldn't have moved to Vermont without the subsidies, Vermont was also one of the few states to either grow more quickly or lose population less quickly in 2019–2020 than in 2018–2019.[344] The subsidies, combined with Vermont's low COVID infection rates and high prevalence of vacation homes, may have induced more people to become permanent residents amid the pandemic.[345]

In many cases, interest in these relocation incentive programs far outstrips the number of people who actually receive the relocation subsidies. For example, Tulsa, Oklahoma, a city of 400,000 people, has received more than 20,000 applications for its relocation incentive program since 2018.[346] Northwest Arkansas, population 530,000, has received more than 24,000 in total, and Topeka, Kansas, population 130,000, received more than 3,500 within its program's first 30 days.[347]

Vermont, Tulsa, Arkansas, and Topeka are far from the only

examples of publicly funded programs attracting residents who are "voting with their feet." In recent years, there has been significant media attention on the large and growing array of such programs around the country, especially in places where the low cost of living may be a particular draw. Figure 3 describes almost two dozen of these programs, the maximum subsidy per household, and the target of the subsidy (student loans, housing, etc.).

**Figure 3: Maximum value of select state and local incentive packages to attract new residents in the U.S.**[348]

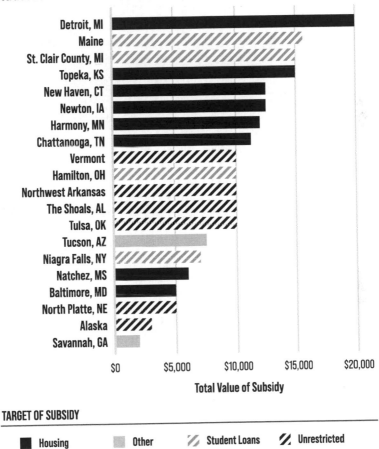

In addition to directly subsidizing moving or housing costs, some cities also offer special products or services to new residents, such as free internet (Tucson), a brand new mountain bike (Northwest Arkansas), or special deals at local businesses (Topeka, Kansas).[349] Many small towns in the Midwest—including Manilla, Iowa; Marne, Iowa; Claremont, Minnesota; and Lincoln, Kansas—are offering to give newcomers plots of vacant land for free.[350] Some cities and states, such as Maine; Kansas; and Hamilton, Ohio, have programs specifically designed to attract young professionals by subsidizing new residents' student loan payments.[351]

## A Push and a Pull in the Same Direction

The academic literature shows that incentive packages are seldom enough to create measurable business migration trends by themselves. Some studies conclude that large companies often receive tax breaks for jobs they would have created regardless.[352] In these cases, it's hard to discount the effect of policies that stifle business activity in corporations' former homes which, combined with efforts other places make to attract these companies, can greatly influence migration decisions.

For example, healthcare corporation McKesson, ranked number 8 on the Fortune 500 as of 2020, moved its global headquarters from California to Texas in 2018, reportedly because of California's high tax rates.[353] An official statement detailing McKesson's move cited Texas's "tremendous support since we opened our Las Colinas campus last April," likely referencing a nearly $10 million grant from the Texas Enterprise Fund to help expand its presence in the state.[354] It's uncertain whether McKesson still would have moved from California to Texas without the grant, but its official statement also said the move would promote "efficiency, collaboration and cost-competitiveness," implying that the contrasting business climate of the two states influenced the company's decision.[355] Such robust investment from the Texas state government also speaks to the lengths to which some states are willing to go to attract economic activity.

The consequences of an expensive, business-unfriendly environment are clear. In 2021, for the first time in its history, California lost a seat in Congress due to a stagnating population.

While there are various causes for California's slower growth, including the state's exorbitant housing costs, many observers have cited economic competition from Texas and other places.[356]

In an example that may hit closer to home in Massachusetts, General Electric moved its headquarters from Fairfield, Connecticut to Boston in 2016 after a $700 million tax hike targeted large corporations and wealthy individuals in the Constitution State.[357] State and local governments in Massachusetts offered GE $145 million in tax breaks as part of the deal, which amounts to more than $180,000 per promised job.[358] While GE paid back the state's $87 million in tax breaks after failing to create enough jobs, the initial offer may have helped push the company to choose Boston over New York, which is 50 miles from its former headquarters and where many of its "peer enterprises" are located.[359] After all, even though tax incentives for specific companies are rarely fruitful economic development strategies, they may still influence business location decisions.

Public agencies are also taking out advertisements in expensive urban enclaves to try to lure people and jobs out-of-state. A recent billboard campaign near Fenway Park by JobsOhio, a state-affiliated economic development group, advertised Ohio's non-existent corporate income tax rate and low cost of living.[360] The City of Miami bought billboards along U.S. Route 101 in San Francisco inviting those looking to move to Miami to contact the Florida city's mayor on Twitter.[361] Similar digital ad campaigns are becoming common on social media.

Even expensive, high tax areas are trying to appeal to corporate migrants with targeted advertisements emphasizing their quality of life, amenities, and existing concentration of talent. In January 2021, Middlesex County, New Jersey launched an ad campaign targeting innovative life science, autonomous vehicle, and food companies looking to relocate from Boston.[362]

While it's too early to assess whether this sort of ad campaign will be effective at bringing investment to New Jersey, whose corporate tax rate is the highest in the nation, such a highly competitive atmosphere for attracting businesses is an insidious backdrop against which to contemplate a graduated tax proposal in Massachusetts, which has historically ranked low on tax and business competitiveness indicators.[363] With cities and states, including other "high-tax, high-talent" ones, throwing billions of dollars into corporate subsidies and advertising each year, the last thing Massachusetts needs is to give its major businesses another reason to leave the state.

In an increasingly nationalized and globalized economy, cities and states will go to great lengths to attract firms, capital, and people to their jurisdictions. But failing to maintain a pro-business climate would be making a dangerous wager on the opposite approach: that the appeal of Massachusetts as a place to live, work, and do business is great enough that it can be taken for granted.

As traditional job centers like Boston and Springfield are facing a renewed vulnerability to out-migration from companies and individuals alike, such an approach would be nothing short of irresponsible.

Among the reasons that it is already a good time to move out of Massachusetts are:

- Pandemic-related mandates, accommodations from employers, and new technologies have made it as feasible as ever for many employees to work remotely
- Rising costs of living, especially home prices, have strained the wallets of the middle class and created an unfriendly environment for young people looking to set down roots
- Other, especially non-metropolitan, cities and states have intensified efforts to lure residents and employers away from major job centers with tax breaks and subsidy packages

On top of the challenges Massachusetts already faces trying to keep talented workers and innovative companies, passing irresponsible tax and regulatory policies would induce even more people and businesses to move elsewhere. Ultimately, this impacts not only the people and businesses who choose to leave, but also the workers employed at these businesses. The recent proliferation of relocation incentive programs and subsidies targeted at both families and businesses signifies a direct incentive for the middle class to leave as well.

While Massachusetts can't stop other states from creating subsidy programs, it can create a tax and regulatory environment that is more attuned to the needs of businesses and individual households throughout the Commonwealth. Fundamentally, this means rejecting tax hikes and business restraints that play right into the hands of those trying to lure people and jobs out of the state.

Besides elaborate benefits programs, Massachusetts' neighboring states have also used more traditional stimulus measures in an attempt to attract residents and businesses in recent years. In fact, just as the Massachusetts legislature was considering the proposed graduated income tax ahead of approving it for the 2022 ballot, the New Hampshire legislature passed a tax cut that is only likely to exacerbate any impact the surtax will have. We discuss this tax cut further in the next section.

## New Hampshire Just Cut Taxes — Will Massachusetts Raise Them?

As Massachusetts voters weigh an amendment to the state constitution to enact a surtax on million-dollar earners, they should be cognizant of how the policies of other states could interact with the tax hike to encourage an exodus of jobs and capital. We've already discussed at length the draw that Florida has had for Massachusetts' tax filers, with the Commonwealth having lost $9.6 billion in adjusted gross income to the Sunshine State between 1993 and 2018. But we should be especially aware of policies adopted in proximate jurisdictions. New Hampshire is a neighboring state that has already benefited from out-migration from Massachusetts to the tune of more than $426 million in taxable income in 2019 alone.[364]

New Hampshire is, by most measures, a low-tax state, increasing its appeal as a destination for domestic migrants.[365] Despite having no tax on personal earned income, it has a 5% tax rate on interest and dividends. However, a budget amendment enacted in June 2021 will eliminate the interest and dividends tax by 2027, contributing to a divergence in tax policy between New Hampshire and many of its neighbors that proponents say would help "attract an increasingly mobile workforce and entrepreneurial base."[366]

## Diverging Paths on Tax Policy

When New Hampshire's tax cut is fully implemented, the timing couldn't be worse for Massachusetts, which has already experienced increased vulnerability to an exodus of workers and businesses as a result of the work-from-home phenomenon during the COVID-19 pandemic.[367] New Hampshire's tax cut, combined with a mirroring income tax increase in Massachusetts, could accelerate the long-standing trend of income and capital flowing from Massachusetts to less expensive states.[368]

The combination of the graduated income tax and New Hampshire's fiscal belt-tightening seems particularly poised to lure financial services jobs out of the Commonwealth, given that Massachusetts' surtax would apply to capital gains and New Hampshire's tax cut applies solely to interest and dividends. In turn, the financial services industry is a crucial backer of high-tech startups that have catalyzed the Bay State's innovation economy in recent years while also creating demand for low-skill service jobs that benefit workers of all stripes.[369]

This economic misstep is not just theoretical. A divergence in income tax rates between Massachusetts and its competitor states seems to have accelerated the direction of capital flows in recent years. In the notable example of Connecticut, the flow has benefited Massachusetts, as we discussed in the opening chapter. Connecticut's top marginal income tax rate increased from 4.5% in 2003 to 6.99% in 2018, even while Massachusetts's top rate decreased from 5.6 to 5.1 % over the same period.[370] Overall, Connecticut personal income tax hikes have taken effect in 2004, 2009, 2012, and 2016. Massachusetts personal income tax cuts have taken effect in 2004, 2012, 2014, 2016, 2019, and 2020.[371]

At the same time, taxpayers migrating between Connecticut and Massachusetts brought increasing amounts of wealth to the Bay State. As shown in Figure 4, by 2019, households that moved from Connecticut to Massachusetts made nearly $195 million more in adjusted gross income (AGI) than households that moved from Massachusetts to Connecticut that same year. This is a reversal of the flow that predominated before Connecticut's spate of tax increases. As recently as 2004, interstate migration between Connecticut and its northern neighbor brought more net wealth to Connecticut.

**Figure 4: Net AGI migration from Connecticut to Massachusetts, 2004–2019**

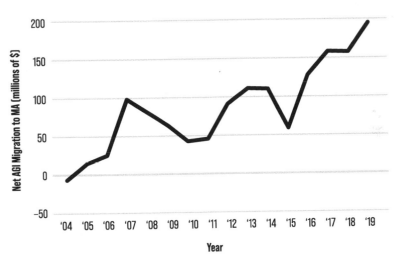

This reversal in fortune for the Constitution State provides a compelling explanation for Connecticut's perennial budget deficits: even as tax rates were increasing, the amount of taxable income was growing slowly due to out-migration. This fact is, in turn, reflected in state coffers: between fiscal years 2008 and 2020, the state budget grew by 63% in Massachusetts, and just 22% in Connecticut.[372]

Unlike Connecticut, Rhode Island provides an example of a state that has cut taxes even more aggressively than Massachusetts over the last 25 years. For most of the 1990s, income tax rates in Rhode Island were determined as a percentage of federal income tax payments, with different brackets paying between 25 and 32.5% of federal taxes (or, at a 39.6% federal rate, between 9.9 and 12.9% of income).[373] These rates gradually converged to

25% by 2002.[374] A 2011 tax reform knocked the 9.9% top marginal rate to 5.99%, where it remains as of 2021.[375] This makes for a particularly important test for the link between tax policy and wealth migration because, unlike in Massachusetts and Connecticut, the major tax changes were concentrated in one year — 2011 — rather than occurring incrementally.

**Figure 5: Net AGI migration from Rhode Island to Massachusetts, 2004-2019**

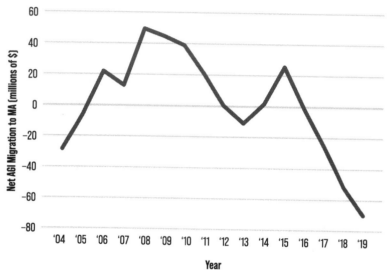

Once a mixed picture, Massachusetts now routinely loses more wealth to Rhode Island than The Ocean State does to Massachusetts, and in recent years the gap has only grown. In Figure 5, note that the trend was increasingly for migrants to favor Massachusetts over Rhode Island until the Great Recession, and the Rhode Island state assembly voted in 2010 to cut the top tax rate to 5.99% in 2011. While Rhode Island's top income tax rate is still higher than that of Massachusetts, that barrier has been lowered enough that other factors — such as the cost of living — have likely kicked in and contributed to Rhode Island's recent edge.

## Figure 6: Net AGI migration from New York to Massachusetts, 2004-2019

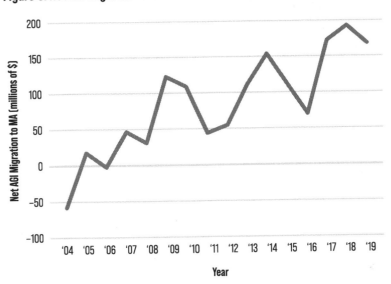

Conversely, other northeastern states have raised taxes over the past couple of decades, including New York and New Jersey. The Empire State first raised its top personal income tax rate to nearly 9% in 2009 before adopting a true "millionaires tax" in 2012.[376] Meanwhile, New Jersey recently doubled down on its 2004 millionaires tax by creating a new tax bracket for those making at least $5 million per year that took effect in 2019. Both display a very similar trend as Connecticut, with increasing amounts of wealth migration to the Bay State in recent years (see Figures 6 and 7).

AGI migration to Massachusetts even from states outside the Northeast closely tracks with tax policy changes. In a situation most immediately comparable to that of New Hampshire, Tennessee phased out its own investment income tax starting in 2016. While migrants' wealth has consistently flowed from Massachusetts to Tennessee over the last decade and a half, the magnitude has increased enormously in recent years. Between 2016 and 2017, when Tennessee's governor signed the law to eliminate the tax, net AGI migration from Massachusetts to

Tennessee more than quadrupled to over $30 million (see Figure 8), even though Tennessee is hundreds of miles away from the Bay State.[377]

Figure 7: Net AGI migration from New Jersey to Massachusetts, 2004–2019

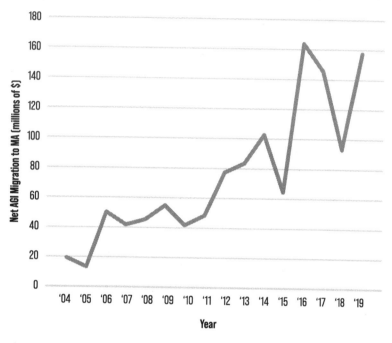

Meanwhile, much of New Hampshire shares a job market with eastern Massachusetts, making it especially appealing for businesses and individuals to move across state lines if the surtax passes. And contrary to Cristobal Young's work, which we dissected in Chapter 5, recent academic research demonstrates that the wealthy are highly responsive to tax changes, whether via physical migration, "shifting" earned income to unearned income, or otherwise.[378] Further, IRS data show that, in 2018, Massachusetts taxpayers who would be subject to the surtax reported $1.87 billion in interest and $4.23 billion in dividends.[379] These facts, combined with the continued divergence of tax policy between New Hampshire and Massachusetts, could reduce the Bay State's tax base, as well as deter talented workers and innovative employers from setting down roots here, if the surtax is passed.

If Massachusetts' surtax proposal is passed, the Bay State would have a marginal income tax rate as high as 9% (and up to 16% for short-term capital gains), while in the Granite State it would be 0%. This discrepancy could prove dangerous in the long-run as Massachusetts seeks a full recovery from COVID-19, especially in an era of remote work.

**Figure 8: Net AGI migration from Tennessee to Massachusetts, 2004–2019**

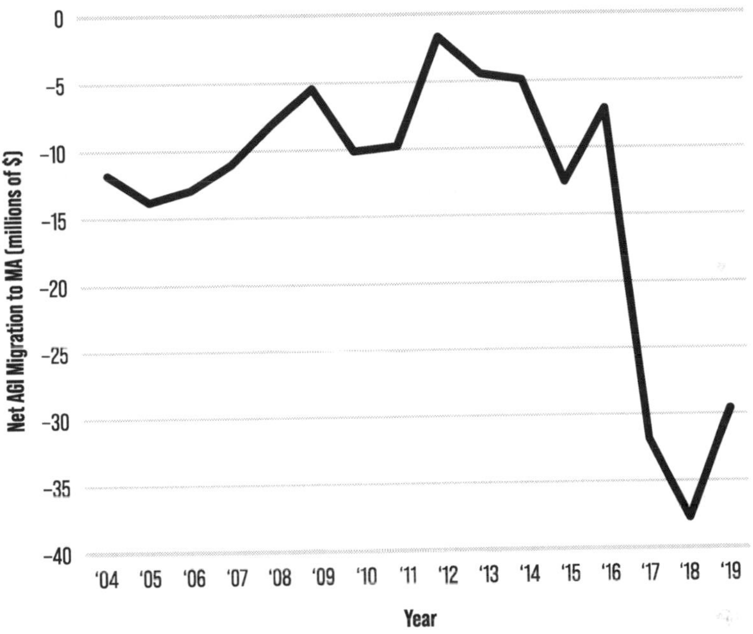

In tandem with tax restraint in recent decades, Massachusetts state revenues have grown much faster than those of neighboring states. Our economy has flourished, in part due to competitive advantages over other cold, expensive places like New York and New Jersey. Wealthy residents of these places have increasingly voted with their feet to move to Massachusetts, bringing jobs and tax dollars with them. Before considering the surtax proposal in 2022, Massachusetts voters should heed a version of an old adage: we're already beating high-tax places. Why join them?

And though this question would be a valid one at any time,

it has become increasingly urgent in light of the 2017 federal Tax Cuts and Jobs Act, which included a cap on the state and local tax (SALT) deduction filers can take on their federal taxes. Absent the SALT deduction, any increase in state tax rates will only magnify the impact on affected taxpayers. We explore this in the next section.

## The SALT Cap Will Also Accelerate Tax Flight from Massachusetts

When Congress enacted the Tax Cuts and Jobs Act of 2017 (TCJA), it altered the economic landscape surrounding the surtax petition that Massachusetts voters will consider in November 2022. The TCJA placed a $10,000 limit on deductions of state income and local property taxes (SALT) on federal individual tax returns, effective for tax years 2018 to 2025. By limiting the deductibility of state and local taxes on federal tax returns, the TCJA raised taxes on filers who itemize deductions, who have disproportionately high incomes.

Notably, much of the existing literature that claims the wealthy do not move in response to tax changes predates the TCJA, which, by capping the SALT deduction, gave those who itemize deductions a stronger incentive to leave high-tax states. When proponents originally advanced the surtax in Massachusetts in 2015, they did so before adoption of the federal SALT deduction limit. Despite this significant change to the federal tax code and its potential to exacerbate the impacts of a tax hike in Massachusetts, the surtax amendment's language remained completely unchanged between the 2015 version submitted by Raise Up Massachusetts and the 2018 version filed by members of the Massachusetts legislature.

### A Whole New Tax Form

The SALT deduction limit came into effect in tax year 2018 in the form of two new lines, 5(d) and 5(e), on I.R.S. Schedule A (Form 1040). In line 5(d), taxpayers enter the total of taxes paid, including state and local income taxes, sales taxes, real estate taxes, and personal property taxes. In line 5(e), taxpayers enter the smaller of line 5(d) or $10,000, as shown in Figure 1.

Taxpayers with Adjusted Gross Incomes (AGI) in excess of $1 million paid an average of $284,050 in state and local taxes in 2018. The SALT deduction limit reduces their deductions to $10,000 (see Figure 9).

**Figure 9: Example of revised Schedule A including $10,000 SALT limitation, introduced in tax year 2018**[380]

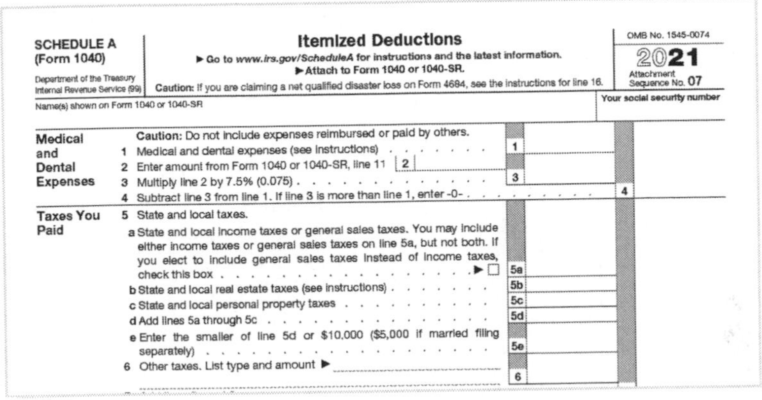
SCHEDULE A (Form 1040)
Department of the Treasury Internal Revenue Service (99)

**Itemized Deductions**
▶ Go to *www.irs.gov/ScheduleA* for instructions and the latest information.
▶ Attach to Form 1040 or 1040-SR.
Caution: If you are claiming a net qualified disaster loss on Form 4684, see the instructions for line 16.

OMB No. 1545-0074
2021
Attachment Sequence No. 07

Name(s) shown on Form 1040 or 1040-SR | Your social security number

**Medical and Dental Expenses**
Caution: Do not include expenses reimbursed or paid by others.
1 Medical and dental expenses (see instructions) . . . . . . . . 1
2 Enter amount from Form 1040 or 1040-SR, line 11 | 2 |
3 Multiply line 2 by 7.5% (0.075) . . . . . . . . . . . . . . 3
4 Subtract line 3 from line 1. If line 3 is more than line 1, enter -0- . . . . . . . . . 4

**Taxes You Paid**
5 State and local taxes.
a State and local income taxes or general sales taxes. You may include either income taxes or general sales taxes on line 5a, but not both. If you elect to include general sales taxes instead of income taxes, check this box . . . . . . . . . . . . . . . . . ▶ ☐ 5a
b State and local real estate taxes (see instructions) . . . . . . . . 5b
c State and local personal property taxes . . . . . . . . . . 5c
d Add lines 5a through 5c . . . . . . . . . . . . . . 5d
e Enter the smaller of line 5d or $10,000 ($5,000 if married filing separately) . . . . . . . . . . . . . . 5e
6 Other taxes. List type and amount ▶ 6

IRS data demonstrate the financial impact of the SALT deduction limit. Prior to passage of the TCJA, U.S. taxpayers took $624.1 billion in SALT deductions on federal returns, an average deduction of $13,395 per return. In tax year 2018, taxpayers took $147.0 billion in SALT deductions, a drop of 76.4% in total deductions, with an average deduction of $8,432 per return (see Figure 10). The number of U.S. taxpayers claiming itemized SALT deductions dropped from 46.6 million in tax year 2017 to 17.4 million in tax year 2018, with a corresponding increase in taxpayers claiming the increased standardized deduction authorized by the TCJA.[381]

While the SALT deduction limit reduced the average deduction of all taxpayers who itemized by 37.1% (from $13,395 to $8,432), it had a much greater impact on high income taxpayers. Prior to passage of the TCJA, taxpayers with Adjusted Gross Incomes (AGIs) of $1 million or more in the U.S. took SALT deductions totaling $128.3 billion on federal returns, an average of $281,916 per return. After the SALT deduction limit took effect in tax year 2018, total SALT deductions these taxpayers took dropped by 96.9% to $4.0 billion, or an average of $9,856 per return. The number of U.S. taxpayers with AGI over $1 million claiming itemized SALT deductions dropped from 455,310 in tax year 2017 to 406,120 in tax year 2018, with a corresponding increase in taxpayers claiming the increased standardized deduction authorized by the TCJA.[382]

**Figure 10: Average SALT deduction taken before and after enactment of TCJA by income category[383]**

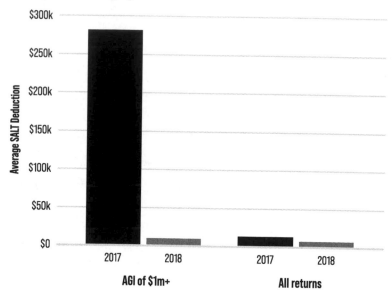

Figure 10 compares the average SALT deduction taken by U.S. taxpayers who itemized deductions in tax years 2017 and 2018 with the average SALT deduction taken by taxpayers with AGIs of $1 million or more in tax years 2017 and 2018.[384]

In 2017, before the TCJA became effective, 97.6% of the 18,090 Massachusetts taxpayers with AGIs of $1 million or more took deductions for state and local taxes totaling $4.02 billion, an average of $227,471 per return. Once the TCJA became effective in tax year 2018, 75.9% of 20,040 Massachusetts taxpayers with AGIs of $1 million or more took deductions for state and local taxes, while the others opted to take the standardized deduction.

Of the high income taxpayers who itemized deductions, total SALT deductions dropped from $4.02 billion in tax year 2017 to $152 million in tax year 2018, a reduction of 96.2%. The average SALT deduction dropped from $227,471 to $9,984.

In June 2019, the Joint Committee on Taxation of the U.S. Congress estimated that 52.2% of the negative tax impact of the SALT deduction limit is borne by taxpayers with AGIs of $1 million or more, which constitutes $40.4 billion of the total of $77.4 billion (see Figure 11).[385]

**Figure 11: Share of tax burden from SALT limitation by income category, Tax Year 2019**[386]

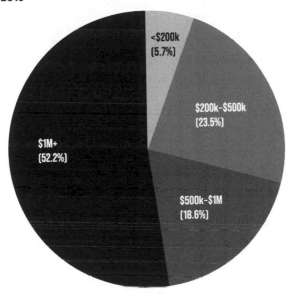

## The Political Fallout

A large contingent of Congressional Democrats, predominantly from states most adversely impacted by the SALT deduction limit, has been working to repeal it, but it won't be easy to do so without a fight, according to Jonathan Traub, tax policy leader of the Washington national tax practice at Deloitte Tax LLP. "Progressives say that full SALT deductibility is a giveaway to the wealthiest of the wealthy, while governors cry about wealthy residents leaving their states and losing their tax base."[387] In April

2021, seven governors of high-tax states signed an open letter urging President Biden to remove the cap on the SALT deduction imposed under the Tax Cuts and Jobs Act.[388]

Larry Summers, former Treasury Secretary and former president of Harvard University, warned on April 9th that New York's proposed millionaire's tax will backfire without congressional repeal of the SALT deduction limit, sending New York into a "downward spiral."[389] This likely alludes to the economic and fiscal impact of the tax base erosion, revenue volatility, and disinvestment associated with such tax increases.

Massachusetts is already acknowledged as being one of the states most affected by the SALT deduction limit. According to a study published by the Rockefeller Institute of Government, Massachusetts had the fourth worst "SALT burden" of the 50 states and D.C. in tax year 2019.[390] A UMass Donahue Center study concluded that the $10,000 cap on deductibility under the TCJA "will make it more difficult for Massachusetts to maintain their prior tax structures. Massachusetts will face greater tax competition from lower-tax neighboring states, particularly New Hampshire. The most productive areas… are particularly hard hit. The result will be a decline in national competitiveness."[391]

Other states, however, may have something to gain from the cap on the SALT deduction. According to Florida real estate developer Nitin Motwani, "SALT has been the No. 1 theme when we speak with finance companies about relocating or opening branch offices in Miami."[392] In January 2020, a Bank of America analysis found that lower-tax states gained $32 billion more in adjusted gross income than higher-tax states in 2018, nearly twice the average amount since 2005.[393] Financial Advisor Magazine later called the Bank of America report the "hardest evidence yet" that the 2017 tax cuts, and specifically the SALT deduction cap, are disproportionately hurting states like Massachusetts and New York.[394]

*Bloomberg News* reported on July 28, 2021 that New York City mayoral Democratic nominee Eric Adams likewise has grave concerns over the SALT deduction cap. Adams "told a group of House lawmakers that the limit on the state and local tax deduction enacted in 2017 is a top issue harming the city, according to two congressional aides familiar with the conversation."[395]

But the limit on SALT deductions has met friends as well as foes across the aisle. When President Biden entered office, some presumed the administration would attempt to repeal the limit on SALT deductions.[396] However, it is uncertain whether this will come to fruition, as SALT cap relief comes with a heavy price tag, especially as the Biden administration is aiming to bolster environmental and social-welfare programs.[397] Experts hypothesize that a partial repeal is the most likely course of action for the immediate future.[398]

As of this writing Congress has come to agreement on legislation to repeal or amend the SALT deduction cap. On November 19, 2021 the House voted 220 to 213 to approve H.R. 5376, the $1.75 trillion Build Back Better budget reconciliation bill, along partisan lines. The bill includes a provision to increase the $10,000 SALT cap to $80,000 and extend its life by six more years, with the cap returning to $10,000 in 2031. In the Senate, where Democrats hold a razor-thin majority , two key senators have said that they will offer a revised version of the SALT cap that places an income limit on the House version of the bill. Senate Budget Committee Chairman, Vermont Independent Senator Bernie Sanders, favors an income limit of $400,000 and New Jersey Democrat Bob Menendez favors $550,000.[399]

If Congress passes the Build Back Better Act with an income limit on eligibility for an amended SALT deduction of less than $1 million, it will have no impact on taxpayers in Massachusetts subject to the proposed surtax on income of $1 million or more.

And even if Congress increases the SALT deduction cap from $10,000 to $80,000 without an income limit, the rollback may only be temporary. As of November 2021, different proposals from House Democrats raise the cap through either 2030 or 2031.[400] Thus, such a policy would do little to change the impact of the SALT cap on the proposed Massachusetts surtax in the long run. For Massachusetts, this means treating tax hikes during the pandemic recovery period with the utmost caution.

## Massachusetts Offers a Workaround

While efforts to address the impact of the SALT deduction limit at the federal level are uncertain, Massachusetts, along with other states, has established a workaround for pass-through entities. The Massachusetts FY 2022 budget included outside Section 39 — entitled "Taxation of Pass-Through Entities (PTEs)."[401]

Section 39 is intended to lessen the impact of the $10,000 SALT deduction limit on federal taxes paid by Massachusetts taxpayers who report income from pass-through entities. These PTEs can include S corporations, partnerships, and LLCs. Under Section 39, an eligible PTE may elect to pay an excise on its income taxable in Massachusetts at a rate of 5%, qualifying members to be eligible for a tax credit on Massachusetts tax returns equal to 90% of their share of excise paid by the PTE. Qualified members of PTEs include natural persons, trusts, and estates. Governor Baker has proposed the credit be 100% of the excise paid, which is why he refused to sign outside Section 39 at the time he signed the budget.

Under the legislature's proposal, if a PTE elects to use the Section 39 workaround, the Massachusetts Department of Revenue (DOR) will receive more in total revenue from the PTE and its members than it otherwise would have received. This is due to the PTE paying the excise, and members paying a 5% tax on the 10% of pass-through income that is not offset by the 90% tax credit. Therefore, the DOR will receive from PTEs electing to use the SALT cap workaround a total of 5.5% of entity taxable income, 5% excise from the entity, and 0.5% income tax from the member. That is, unless the DOR determines that the entity-level tax payment reduces the owner's distributive share of income for MA tax purposes.

The Governor's proposed amendment, setting the credit at 100% of the excise paid, was filed in the House of Representatives on August 5, 2021. In October, however, the legislature overrode Governor Baker's veto and passed the 90% SALT tax credit into law.[402]

Eleven months earlier, in November 2020, the IRS issued an advisory greenlighting "SALT cap workarounds." It announced that future IRS guidance would provide that taxes paid by a partnership or S corporation to a state, a political subdivision of a state, or the District of Columbia would be recognized as legitimate deductible expenses on PTE federal tax returns. This is applicable without regard to whether liability for the income tax is the result of an election by the entity, or whether shareholders receive a deduction, exclusion, credit, or other tax benefit that is based on their share of the amount paid by the partnership or S corporation to satisfy its income tax liability.

The federal government does not require PTEs to pay federal taxes on net income; instead, PTE members pay taxes on their proportionate share of income passed-through by the PTE entity. By allowing a deductible expense at the entity level of a 5% excise paid to the Massachusetts DOR, the IRS effectively lifts the SALT deduction cap on PTE income on federal tax returns. Analysis of Internal Revenue Service data from tax year 2018 shows that 33% of the income of Massachusetts taxpayers with AGIs of $1 million or more came from partnerships and S corporations.[403]

It is important to note, however, that, though the state and federal workarounds for PTEs described here will help reduce some of the burden on Massachusetts taxpayers due to the SALT deduction cap, they will not diminish the amount of surtax payments Massachusetts taxpayers will owe the DOR if the graduated income tax is approved by voters. This is due to the language of the proposed amendment that states: "there shall be an additional tax of 4% on that portion of *annual taxable income* in excess of $1,000,000 (one million dollars) reported on any return related to those taxes."[404] Outside Section 39 does not change the amount of taxable income that a pass-through entity is responsible for reporting to its members as their proportionate share of taxable income. It appears that neither the Section 39 tax credit nor the taxpayer's state tax liability are relevant to the proposed constitutional amendment because the additional 4% surtax is charged by calculating the total amount of annual taxable income, not the amount of taxes due on that income.

## Two Tax Hikes Join Forces

While the proposed surtax would make Massachusetts' top nominal income tax rate the sixth highest in the nation, its effective tax rate could actually rank higher because of its high "SALT burden."[405]

The previously unlimited SALT deduction essentially reduced aggregated taxes paid by allowing taxpayers to deduct state taxes against federal income. According to the estimate made by the Massachusetts Department of Revenue prior to adoption of the federal SALT deduction limit, the average Massachusetts taxpayer who would become subject to the proposed surtax was expected to pay $160,786 in state income taxes in 2019.[406] At the top federal tax rate of 37%, that taxpayer would have received an after-tax benefit of $59,491 on his or her federal taxes as a result of the unlimited SALT deduction of $160,786 of state income taxes paid by him or her (i.e. 37% x $160,786 = $59,491).[407] This $59,491 benefit had the effect of reducing the average state income tax paid by taxpayers in this income category, when aggregated with the federal SALT deduction, from $160,786 to $101,295. After the SALT deduction was capped at $10,000, the average tax savings from the SALT deduction among those who itemize dropped from $59,491 to $3,700, or 37% of $10,000. Thus, the SALT deduction limit increased the average aggregate income tax paid by Massachusetts taxpayers with incomes of more than $1 million from $101,295 to $157,086, after taking the SALT deduction into account. This represents the effect of the SALT deduction limit prior to consideration of the proposed surtax.

But the combined effect of the proposed surtax and the SALT deduction limit is far greater. The DOR estimated that a total of $47.1 billion of income would become subject to the surtax in tax year 2019 if the proposal were enacted.[408] This represented an average of $2,407,240 of income per affected taxpayer who would owe, on average, $96,290 in surtax payments.

## Figure 12: Average net Massachusetts income tax among millionaires after federal tax savings due to the SALT deduction, 2019

|  | Pre-Surtax/ Pre-SALT Cap | Pre-Surtax/ Post-SALT Cap | Post-Surtax/ Pre-SALT CAP | Post-Surtax/ Post-SALT Cap |
|---|---|---|---|---|
| Average AGI of MA taxpayer with AGI of $1M or more | $3,407,240 | $3,407,240 | $3,407,240 | $3,407,240 |
| Average MA income tax owed | $160,786 | $160,786 | $254,355 | $254,355 |
| Percentage increase in MA income tax on all income from amount due pre-surtax, pre-SALT cap | N/A | 0.0% | 58.2% | 58.2% |
| Average tax savings due to SALT deduction (at 37% tax rate) | $59,491 | $3,700 | $94,111 | $3,700 |
| Average MA income tax less benefit of federal SALT deduction | $101,295 | $157,086 | $160,244 | $250,655 |
| Percentage increase in MA income tax on all income less benefit of federal SALT deduction from pre-surtax, pre-SALT cap | N/A | 55.1% | 58.2% | 147.5% |
| Average MA income tax after SALT deduction as share of average AGI | 3.0% | 4.6% | 4.7% | 7.4% |

According to tax revenue estimates prepared by the Massachusetts Department of Revenue (DOR) in 2015, the average state income tax paid by a taxpayer earning at least $1 million in tax year 2019 was expected to increase from $160,786 to $254,355 if the surtax were enacted, an increase of 58.2%, not counting the deductibility of SALT payments on federal taxes.[409] But when the TCJA's cap on SALT deductions is included, the relative increase is much larger, 147.5%, from $101,295, the average aggregate income tax paid by Massachusetts taxpayers with incomes of more than $1 million with no SALT deduction limit in place, to $250,655 with the SALT deduction limit (see Figure 12).

The limitation on the deductibility of SALT expenses would be offset in whole or in part by other elements of the TCJA that impact taxpayers differently depending upon specific components of their tax returns. These elements include a reduction in the top marginal tax rate from 39.6% to 37% for couples filing jointly, a reduction in rates in lower tax brackets, an exemption of up to 20% of income from pass-through entities such as LLCs and Subchapter S corporations, amendments to the alternative minimum tax (AMT), and the repeal of the Pease Limitation on itemized deductions.[410] However, unlike the SALT deduction cap, there's not much evidence that these changes have disproportionately affected Massachusetts taxpayers, as opposed to those in other states. Thus, while the TCJA reduced federal tax obligations for most Americans, it also made Massachusetts a relatively less attractive place to live, work, and do business compared to other states.

As further evidence of how the SALT deduction limit disadvantages Massachusetts, consider that in 2017, the value of the SALT deduction for Massachusetts taxpayers was equivalent to 6.5% of the state's adjusted gross income, but to U.S. taxpayers, it was just 5.6% of national AGI. By 2018, the Tax Cuts and Jobs Act had reduced these figures to 1.2% and 1.1%, respectively, much closer to parity.[411] Thus, what used to be a tax code provision that gave Massachusetts residents much more of a tax break than many other Americans now confers similar benefits to all. While this may be more fair, it could also make Massachusetts taxpayers more likely to leave under the graduated income tax, as the federal tax code now does little to mitigate the burden on residents of high-tax states.

As we noted above, the proposed tax increase would make Massachusetts' top nominal tax rate the sixth highest in the country at 9%. However, its effective tax rate could rank even higher, not just because of its high SALT burden, but because Massachusetts does not allow taxpayers to take many itemized deductions offered by the five states whose tax rates would nominally be higher than Massachusetts' proposed surtax. Those states include California (13.3%), Hawaii (11%), New Jersey (10.75%), Oregon (9.9%), and Minnesota (9.85%).[412] Except for New Jersey, all of the states with top income tax rates nominally higher than those Massachusetts would enact under the surtax proposal, allow taxpayers to itemize deductions. California, Hawaii, Oregon, and Minnesota allow their taxpayers to deduct home mortgage interest and local property taxes, while Massachusetts does not.[413] Oregon allows taxpayers a deduction of up to $6,950 for federal income taxes paid in prior years, while Massachusetts does not.[414]

During the years-long process to get the surtax proposal on the ballot in Massachusetts, the federal government placed a hard cap of $10,000 on its state and local tax deduction, further exposing households in high-tax states to the effects of interstate tax competition. This unforeseen change in the federal tax code had the effect of turning what would have been a 58 percent increase in average state income tax payments among Massachusetts millionaires, from $160,786 to $254,355, into what is essentially a 147 percent increase when the federal SALT limitation is included in the calculation. This substantial change should be taken into consideration by voters when they contemplate approving the surtax proposal. As noted by prominent economist Larry Summers, a so-called millionaire's tax has the real potential to send a state into a downward spiral when exacerbated by the SALT limitation. Massachusetts has already been identified as the fourth hardest hit state by the SALT deduction. Doubling the average net income tax in Massachusetts, after taking into account the SALT deduction, risks following in the footsteps of states like Connecticut and Illinois, whose tax policies have contributed to perennial budget gaps and prolonged economic stagnation.

Chapter 7

# Conclusion

This is no time to threaten Massachusetts' prospects for an immediate economic recovery from a once-in-a-century pandemic. The long-term economic competitiveness of the Commonwealth rests on a precarious point. Unfortunately, Massachusetts lawmakers voted to send the proposed constitutional amendment to the statewide ballot in 2022. Now it's up to voters to recognize the potential dangers posed by the ballot initiative and the misinformation spread by its proponents:

1. **The tax policies of Connecticut and California are instructive.** Our neighbor to the south provides strong evidence of the likely result of adopting the amendment: Connecticut is still recovering from more than a decade of "soak the rich" policies. Between 2008 and 2020, it ranked 49th among the states in both private-sector wage and job growth. Many larger companies left the state. By contrast, Massachusetts, whose income tax rate declined over the same period that Connecticut was hiking its rates, generated budget growth of 63%. And in California, the exodus of companies and jobs out of state eroded 61% of would-be new revenues by just the second year following its own graduated income tax initiative. In the pages of this book, we show that most taxpayers who left Massachusetts in recent years moved to low-tax states like Florida and New Hampshire.

2. **There's no assurance that the funding would go toward what the amendment's proponents say it will.** We could be looking at the biggest shell game in the Commonwealth's history. The amendment does not guarantee that any revenues generated from the new tax would increase

overall spending on education and transportation, as supporters claim. Lawyers on both sides of the 2018 Supreme Judicial Court case, and even the SJC's chief justice at the time, all agreed that it would not violate the amendment if any new revenue for education and transportation generated by the surtax was counterbalanced by diverting funds previously dedicated to those priorities. This sort of "shell game" is exactly what happened in California. After the 2012 tax hike "to fund education," funding increased only to the degree required by existing state funding quotas. The remainder helped to inflate the state's payroll, which grew at twice the national average between 2012 and 2020. And Massachusetts has no such funding quotas for either education or transportation, meaning that 100% of the new money could be used to replace funds diverted to other priorities. The fact that the Massachusetts legislature has twice rejected amendment proposals to direct new revenues to education and transportation speaks for itself.

3. **The tax would hamper the competitiveness of the Massachusetts economy.** For the financial services industry, which employed more than 191,000 people in 2019 in Massachusetts, with more than three-quarters of those jobs located in Greater Boston, the tax would be devastating. If passed, the surtax will give Massachusetts the highest short-term capital gains tax rate in the nation and the highest long-term capital gains tax rate in New England. For investors, there is a particularly punitive aspect of a graduated state income tax proposal: In Massachusetts, unlike at the federal level, capital gains can push you into a higher tax bracket.

Pass-through entities would be greatly impacted, particularly subchapter S corporations. In Massachusetts, nearly half of employees at private, for-profit sector firms worked for pass-through entities in 2019. Enactment of the proposed surtax tax would mean that some S corporations, in effect, would pay up to 12% of their taxable income above $1 million to the state — the 5% pass-through personal income tax, the 3% sting tax, and the

4% millionaire's tax.

A partner or member's proportionate share of taxable net income from a pass-through entity is counted in full in determining his or her tax liability, including the tax on income in excess of $1 million that would be subject to the proposed surtax, whether or not the partner or member has received the income in the form of distributions.

4. **Homeowners and business owners, many of whom are one-time millionaires from capital gains resulting from cashing in on home equity or a lifetime of work in advance of retirement, would have their nest-eggs eroded.** Data show that nearly half the capital gains earned in the U.S. from 2007–2012 were from pass-through businesses, another common source of retirement funding. National data from the U.S. Treasury Department show that the majority of taxpayers earning more than $1 million in a year did so only once over a nine-year period. In Massachusetts, 46% of the people who would be affected by the tax — those who earned incomes over $1 million — did so only once in 10 years. 60% did so only once or twice in the 10-year period that ended in 2017.

5. **The number of Massachusetts residents subject to the tax has been understated.** The methodology proponents rely on to ratchet down the number of people paying the new tax ignores the fact that the majority of U.S. households with high net worth, defined as greater than $10 million, earn less than $1 million annually. In fact, almost 60% of households with greater than $10 million in net worth had annual incomes of less than $1 million.[415] Cumulatively, these households have trillions of dollars in unrealized capital gains that may be subject to the graduated income tax upon sale.[416] More insidiously, a tax like the so-called Fair Share Amendment would also deter high-net-worth individuals from moving to Massachusetts in the first place.

While data on the migration patterns of high-net-worth individuals are scarce, the sheer number of people who could potentially be millionaires in a given year by selling a portion of their assets constitutes a vulnerability to tax avoidance. Thus, net worth is a better measure of wealth than prior year income when analyzing migration in response to taxation.

6. **Misinformation abounds in proponents' effort to control the debate.** Raise Up's conclusion is that "our wealthiest residents can clearly afford to pay a little more to fund the investments we all need." But Massachusetts tax policy is already more progressive than in most other states. The public employee unions that originally proposed the tax claim that the Commonwealth's tax system is regressive, citing the Institute on Taxation and Economic Policy (ITEP). But ITEP finds that Massachusetts taxes are materially more progressive than the average of the 49 other states and Washington, D.C.

7. **The tax proposal is particularly risky because the pandemic drastically changed the way we work and live, accelerating wealth and business flight.** Technology is making it easier for individuals to be mobile, and the world of work has shifted dramatically throughout during the pandemic. The proposed constitutional amendment comes just as the rise in telecommuting makes it easier for wealthy taxpayers to live — and pay taxes — anywhere. Massachusetts already loses nearly $1 billion of wealth per year due to residents relocating elsewhere, primarily to low- or no-tax states.

   The same is true of the mobility of businesses. A 2020 Princeton study found that state and local governments lure companies with tax incentives worth at least $30 billion annually. And companies appear to be responding. The migration rate for large firms in the U.S. nearly doubled in less than 20 years between the mid-1990s and early 2010s, well before the pandemic made telecommuting, and the mobility it created, the norm.

8. **States are highly competitive to attract business and residents.** Neighboring New Hampshire is making moves to capitalize on the Commonwealth's tax policies. Despite having no tax on personal earned income, New Hampshire

has a 5% tax rate on interest and dividends. However, a budget amendment enacted in June 2021 will eliminate the interest and dividends tax by 2027, contributing to a divergence in tax policy between New Hampshire and many of its neighbors that proponents say would help "attract an increasingly mobile workforce and entrepreneurial base."[417]

9. **Federal tax policies are accelerating tax flight from Massachusetts.** After the authors of the proposed graduated tax originally submitted their proposal for legislative approval in 2017, the federal government placed a $10,000 limit on the deductibility of state and local taxes on federal returns. This change in the federal tax code has had the effect of turning what would have been a 58 nearly 60 % increase in average state income tax payments among Massachusetts millionaires, from $160,786 to $254,355, into what is essentially a 147% increase when the federal SALT benefit is included in the calculation. As noted by Larry Summers, a so-called millionaire's tax has the real potential to send a state into a downward spiral due to the exacerbating effect of the SALT deduction limit. Massachusetts has already been identified as the 4th hardest hit state by the cap on the SALT deduction.

All this is being contemplated at a time when economic growth is already generating billions in surplus for the state. The Massachusetts state government collected over $5 billion more in tax revenue in Fiscal Year 2021 than they had projected, a massive surplus that represents revenue growth of more than 15% over Fiscal Year 2020. Then, in November 2021, state officials devised a plan to spend nearly $4 billion in one-time federal stimulus payments. Wisely spending the enormous surpluses the Commonwealth will enjoy in the near future is more important than trying to add to them through a tax policy shell game.

And it can start by helping to get the Massachusetts residents who no longer have jobs post-pandemic back to work, in part by ensuring that small businesses and pass-through entities that might employ them are not burdened with additional taxes.

The second priority should be to ensure that the 90% of Massachusetts employees who work in the private sector will benefit from a strong economy a generation from now.

As of September 2021, there are 217,000 residents of the Commonwealth who were working in February 2020 but are now unemployed after the pandemic ravaged Massachusetts' private sector workforce. The proposed amendment may benefit the 3% of the workforce that is employed by the state, but it will do so at the expense of the 90% of the overall employment base that works in the private sector.

If voters approve the measure, it cannot be easily undone. Because it's a consititutional amendment rather than a law, repeal would require approval by two consecutive state legislatures, followed by another statewide referendum.

It is disturbing that ample and clear data and analysis did not hold sway with the legislature. We trust that voters will, as they have so many times in the past, recognize the adverse impact the tax amendment will have on their livelihoods and those of future generations.

# ACKNOWLEDGEMENTS

We are deeply indebted to a number of people whose work made this book possible. First and foremost, attorney Kevin Martin, whose legal expertise and eloquent writing contributed greatly to the substance of our arguments above. Further, Joseph X. Donovan and David Nagel, experts in state and local tax law, were particularly diligent in helping us understand the impacts of the SALT deduction cap on the proposed millionaire's tax.

Much of the IRS data we cite throughout the book was compiled and formatted by Michael Walker of DataMadeUseful. Michael constructed a number of interactive data tools to allow our researchers to explore the prevalence of wealth migration in Massachusetts and other states. This data is now publicly available at https://massirsdatadiscovery.com/.

Mary Connaughton has had a crucial role in guiding the direction of our research at Pioneer Institute since the surtax was first proposed in 2015. She has edited every single policy brief and white paper on the surtax we've released in the last 4 years, which papers were edited and aggregated into this book. She also has hired and coordinated the involvement of contractors, legal experts, and writers in making the book.

Several individuals contributed research on individual chapters or sections of chapters. Liv Leone wrote and edited much of the section on the SALT deduction. Nina Weiss conducted extensive research on the effect of the proposed surtax on pass-through entities. Serena Hajjar examined employment trends among public and private sector agencies in the aftermath of the COVID-19 pandemic.

Much of the editing work for the volume fell on Charlie Chieppo and Caitlin Marple. They are largely the reason this book maintains cohesion, concision, and comprehensibility to the layperson.

Last, but certainly not least, we'd like to thank Jim Stergios, executive director of Pioneer Institute, as well as the Pioneer Institute Board of Directors, for their guidance in focusing the efforts of Pioneer staff and contractors on issues of tax policy and economic opportunity more broadly. It is ultimately the Institute's deeply committed and knowledgeable individuals who make up our internal governance that allow us to do this work.

Sincerely,
Greg, Andrew, and Liam

# Endnotes

1   Katherine Loughead, "State Individual Income Tax Rates and Brackets for 2021," Tax Foundation, February 17, 2021, https://taxfoundation.org/publications/state-individual-income-tax-rates-and-brackets/

2   Phoenix Wealth & Affluent Monitor, "Report: Millionaire Rankings by State — Through Year-End 2019," Phoenix Marketing International, 2020, https://www.phoenixmi.com/learn/report-millionaire-rankings-by-state-through-year-end-2019/

3   United States Bureau of Labor Statistics, "Quarterly Census of Employment and Wages," United States Department of Labor, last updated January 2, 2020, https://data.bls.gov/cew/apps/data_views/data_views.htm#tab=Tables

Connecticut Department of Labor, "Annual Averages — Employment & Wages by Industry (QCEW) — State of Connecticut," State of Connecticut, last updated July 22, 2020, https://www1.ctdol.state.ct.us/lmi/202/202_annualaverage.asp

United States Bureau of Labor Statistics, "Private industry by six-digit NAICS industry and government by level of government, 2008 annual averages: Establishments, employment, and wages, change from 2007," United States Department of Labor, 2008, https://www.bls.gov/cew/publications/employment-and-wages-annual-averages/2008/tables/private-industry-by-six-digit-naics-and-government-by-level-of-government.pdf

4   The Business Council of Fairfield County Foundation, "Connecticut Economic Competitive Diagnosis," April 8, 2016, https://ccea.uconn.edu/wp-content/uploads/sites/968/2016/08/CT-McKinsey-Summary-2016.pdf

5   Thurston Powers, "Where Has All the Money Gone? The 25th Anniversary of Connecticut's Income Tax," Yankee Institute for Public Policy Research, August 22, 2016, https://yankeeinstitute.org/policy_paper/where-has-all-the-money-gone/

6   Ibid.

7   Ibid.

8   Ibid.

9   Ibid.

10  Tami Luhby, "Tax hikes on the way for Connecticut residents," CNN Money, May 6, 2011, https://money.cnn.com/2011/05/04/news/economy/connecticut_raises_taxes/index.htm

11  James, R. Brockway, "United States: Connecticut Budget Bill Raises Taxes For Individuals And Businesses," Withers LLP, June 29, 2015, https://www.withersworldwide.com/en-gb/insight/connecticut-budget-bill-raises-taxes-for-individuals-and-businesses

12  Ibid.

13  Anthony Switajewski & Christopher Buno, "Connecticut Budget — What You Need To Know," Blum Shapiro, July 17, 2019, https://www.blumshapiro.com/insights/connecticut-budget-what-you-need-to-know/

14  Christopher Keating, "Connecticut Fighting To Keep GE Headquarters," The Hartford Courant, November 16, 2015, https://www.courant.com/politics/hc-ge-new-headquarters-1115-20151116-story.html

15  Tax Foundation, "State-Local Tax Burden Rankings FY 2012," January 20, 2016, https://taxfoundation.org/state-local-tax-burden-rankings-fy-2012/.

16  Janelle Cammenga, "Fact and Figures 2020: How Does Your State Compare?" Tax Foundation, February 13, 2020, https://taxfoundation.org/facts-and-figures-2020/

17  Derek Thompson, "What on Earth Is Wrong With Connecticut?" The Atlantic, July 5, 2017, https://www.theatlantic.com/business/archive/2017/07/connecticut-tax-inequality-cities/532623/

18  Marc E. Fitch, "Connecticut still faces billion-dollar budget deficits for 2022 through 2024," Yankee Institute for Public Policy, October 22, 2019, https://yankeeinstitute.org/2019/10/22/connecticut-still-faces-billion-dollar-budget-deficits-for-2022-through-2024/

19  Mac. E. Fitch, "Gov. Lamont relies on Rainy Day Fund, hiring freeze to balance this year's budget," Yankee Institute for Public Policy, October 7, 2020, https://yankeeinstitute.org/2020/10/07/gov-lamont-relies-on-rainy-day-fund-hiring-freeze-to-balance-this-years-budget/

20  Samuel Stebbins, "Which states in the US have the highest tax burdens? Many can be found in North, Northeast," USA Today, last updated April 20, 2020, https://www.usatoday.com/story/money/2020/04/19/taxes-2020-states-with-the-highest-and-lowest-taxes/111555224/

21  United States Bureau of Labor Statistics, "Regional and state employment and unemployment: January 2009," United States Department of Labor, March 11, 2009, https://www.bls.gov/news.release/archives/laus_03112009.pdf

    United States Bureau of Labor Statistics, "State employment and unemployment - March 2020," United States Department of Labor, April 17, 2020, https://www.bls.gov/news.release/archives/laus_04172020.pdf

22  Ibid.

23  Office of the State Comptroller, "Comptroller Lembo Says State On Track To End Fiscal Year 2017 With $107.2-Million Deficit," State of Connecticut, July 3, 2017, https://www.osc.ct.gov/public/news/releases/20170703.html

24  Federal Reserve Economic Database, "All Employees, Total Nonfarm (PAYEMS)," Federal Reserve Bank of St. Louis, last updated November 6, 2020, https://fred.stlouisfed.org/series/PAYEMS

    Federal Reserve Economic Database, "All Employees: Total Nonfarm in Connecticut (CTNA)," Federal Reserve Bank of St. Louis, last updated October 20, 2020, https://fred.stlouisfed.org/series/ctna

25   United States Bureau of Labor Statistics, "Quarterly Census of Employment and Wages," United States Department of Labor, last updated January 2, 2020, https://data.bls.gov/cew/apps/data_views/data_views.htm#tab=Tables

Connecticut Department of Labor, "Annual Averages — Employment & Wages by Industry (QCEW)— State of Connecticut," State of Connecticut, last updated July 22, 2020, https://www1.ctdol.state.ct.us/lmi/202/202_annualaverage.asp

United States Bureau of Labor Statistics, "Private industry by six-digit NAICS industry and government by level of government, 2008 annual averages: Establishments, employment, and wages, change from 2007," United States Department of Labor, 2008, https://www.bls.gov/cew/publications/employment-and-wages-annual-averages/2008/tables/private-industry-by-six-digit-naics-and-government-by-level-of-government.pdf

26   United States Bureau of Labor Statistics, "QCEW State and County Map," United States Department of Labor, https://data.bls.gov/maps/cew/US?period=2020-Q1&industry=10&pos_color=blue&neg_color=orange&chartData=6&ownerType=5&distribution=1&Update=Update#tab1

27   Federal Reserve Economic Database, "Average Hourly Earnings of All Employees, Total Private (CES0500000003)," Federal Reserve Bank of St. Louis, last updated November 6, 2020, https://fred.stlouisfed.org/series/CES0500000003

28   The Business Council of Fairfield County Foundation, "Connecticut Economic Competitive Diagnosis," April 8, 2016, https://ccea.uconn.edu/wp-content/uploads/sites/968/2016/08/CT-McKinsey-Summary-2016.pdf

29   Johnathan Williams, Arthur B. Laffer, & Stephen Moore, "Rich States Poor States Archive," American Legislative Exchange Council, last updated August 12, 2020, https://www.alec.org/periodical/rich-states/

30   Ibid.

31   Marc E. Fitch, "Connecticut in 'economic freefall,' according to study," Yankee Institute for Public Policy, August 4, 2020, https://yankeeinstitute.org/2020/08/04/connecticut-in-economic-freefall-according-to-study/

32   United States Bureau of Labor Statistics, "Quarterly Census of Employment and Wages," United States Department of Labor, last updated January 2, 2020, https://data.bls.gov/cew/apps/data_views/data_views.htm#tab=Tables

Connecticut Department of Labor, "Annual Averages — Employment & Wages by Industry (QCEW) — State of Connecticut," State of Connecticut, last updated July 22, 2020, https://www1.ctdol.state.ct.us/lmi/202/202_annualaverage.asp

United States Bureau of Labor Statistics, "Private industry by six-digit NAICS industry and government by level of government, 2008 annual averages: Establishments, employment, and wages, change from 2007," United States Department of Labor, 2008, https://www.bls.gov/cew/publications/employment-and-wages-annual-averages/2008/tables/private-industry-by-six-digit-naics-and-government-by-level-of-government.pdf

33  Federal Housing Finance Agency, "House Price Index Datasets," 2020,
    https://www.fhfa.gov/DataTools/Downloads/Pages/House-Price-Index-Datasets.
    aspx#qpo

34  Federal Reserve Economic Database, "All-Transactions House Price Index for
    Fairfield County, CT (ATNHPIUS09001A)," Federal Reserve Bank of St. Louis, last
    updated June 24, 2020, https://fred.stlouisfed.org/series/ATNHPIUS09001A

35  Keith M. Phaneuf, "Economist Perna: Connecticut's budget in 'a state of
    emergency,'" CT Mirror, April 2, 2017, https://ctmirror.org/2017/04/02/economist-
    perna-connecticuts-budget-is-in-a-state-of-emergency/

36  Katherine Loughead, "State Individual Income Tax Rates and Brackets for 2020,"
    Tax Foundation, February 4, 2020, https://taxfoundation.org/state-individual-
    income-tax-rates-and-brackets-for-2020/

37  Janelle Camenga, "Does Your State Have an Estate or Inheritance Tax?" Tax
    Foundation, September 2, 2020, https://taxfoundation.org/state-estate-tax-state-
    inheritance-tax-2020/

38  Katherine Loughead, "State Tax Changes Effective January 1, 2021," Tax
    Foundation, January 5, 2021, https://taxfoundation.org/2021-state-tax-changes/

39  Anthony Switajewski & Christopher Buno, "Connecticut Budget — What You Need
    To Know," Blum Shapiro, July 17, 2019, https://www.blumshapiro.com/insights/
    connecticut-budget-what-you-need-to-know/

40  Steve Lohr, "G.E. Is Moving Headquarters to Boston and Itself Into the Digital
    Era," The New York Times, Jan. 13, 2016, https://www.nytimes.com/2016/01/14/
    technology/ge-boston-headquarters.html

    Don Seiffert, "GE's global headcount is down 30% since it moved to Boston,"
    Boston Business Journal, February 25, 2020, https://www.bizjournals.com/boston/
    news/2020/02/25/ges-global-headcount-is-down-30-since-it-moved-
    to.html

41  Greg Ryan, "New book dishes on why GE left Connecticut for Boston,"
    The Springfield Republican, August 1, 2020, https://www.masslive.com/
    boston/2020/08/new-book-dishes-on-why-ge-left-connecticut-for-boston.html

42  Christopher Canthrill, "Connecticut Government Debt Chart,"
    USGovernmentSpending.com, 2020, https://www.usgovernmentspending.com/
    spending_chart_2007_2023CTp_22s2li111mcny_H0sH0l

43  Neil Vigdor, "Officials worried GE might donate its headquarters to university,"
    Connecticut Post, Jan. 3, 2016, http://www.ctpost.com/news/article/Officials-
    worried-GE-might-donate-its-6730628.php

44  Marc E. Fitch, "Loss of top Aetna executives could cost Connecticut $3 million
    in tax revenue," The Yankee Institute for Public Policy, July 13, 2017, http://www.
    yankeeinstitute.org/2017/07/loss-of-top-aetna-executives-could-cost-connecticut-
    3-million-in-tax-revenue/

Jon Chesto, "Why are so many business giants leaving Conn.?" The Boston Globe, Sept. 12, 2017, https://www.bostonglobe.com/business/talking-points/2017/09/12/why-are-many-business-giants-leaving-connecticut/SmlxbJLLRjKUxpeyyl6SSI/story.html

45  Susan Haigh, "Aetna to Leave Connecticut Headquarters for New York City," Associated Press, June 29, 2017, https://www.usnews.com/news/best-states/connecticut/articles/2017-06-29/aetna-to-leave-connecticut-headquarters-for-new-york-city

46  Ibid

47  NBC Connecticut, "CVS Commits to Keeping Aetna Headquarters in Hartford for Next 10 Years," last updated October 4, 2018, https://www.nbcconnecticut.com/news/local/cvs-commits-to-keeping-aetna-headquarters-in-hartford-for-next-10-years/165114/

48  Christopher Keating, "GE, Aetna, Travelers Criticize State Tax Increases," Hartford Courant, June 2, 2015, http://www.courant.com/politics/capitol-watch/hc-lawmakers-debate-revenueestimates-liquor-changes-20150601-story.html.

49  Ibid.

50  Patrick Gleason, "General Electric Shipping Up To Boston, And Connecticut Only Has Itself To Blame," Forbes, Jan. 17, 2016, https://www.forbes.com/sites/patrickgleason/2016/01/17/gedeparture/#748b1e8b50a1.

51  Federal Housing Finance Agency, "House Price Index Datasets," 2020, https://www.fhfa.gov/DataTools/Downloads/Pages/House-Price-Index-Datasets.aspx#qpo

52  Throughout this book, "net AGI migration" refers to the total taxable income of taxpayers who moved from other states to the subject state in a given year *minus* the total taxable income of taxpayers who moved from the subject state to other states that same year.

53  Michael Walker, "US Gross Migration Data Age Income Level," Tableau Public, November 10, 2020, https://public.tableau.com/profile/michael.walker#!/vizhome/US_Gross_Migration_Age_IncomeLevel/DataNotes

54  Ibid.

55  Massachusetts IRS Data Discovery, "State to State Migration by Age and Income," Pioneer Institute for Public Policy Research, 2021, https://massirsdatadiscovery.com/tax-payer-migration/state-to-state-migration-by-age-and-income

United States Census Bureau, "State Population Totals and Components of Change: 2010–2019," U.S. Department of Commerce, last updated April 20, 2021, https://www.census.gov/data/tables/time-series/demo/popest/2010s-state-total.html

56  Susan Haigh, "Connecticut Feels Effect of Drop in Super-Rich Tax Payments," Associated Press, May 7, 2017, https://www.usnews.com/news/best-states/connecticut/articles/2017-05-07/connecticut-feels-effect-of-drop-in-super-rich-tax-payments

57   Keith M. Phaneuf & Clarice Silber, "Do millionaires really leave the state when taxes get higher?" The Hartford Courant, December 26, 2018, https://www.courant.com/politics/hc-pol-millionaires-leaving-ct-1226-20181226-dy2bmxno7fdpnbeeojoowcuwyi-story.html

58   Jim Zebora, "10 Fairfield County billionaires among 400 richest Americans," The Connecticut Post, September 23, 2010, https://www.ctpost.com/local/article/10-Fairfield-County-billionaires-among-400-672290.php#photo-342181

59   Kerry A. Dolan, Chase Peterson-Withorn, & Jennifer Wang, "The Forbes 400 2020," Forbes Magazine, 2020, https://www.forbes.com/forbes-400/

60   Michelle Celarier, "You Make $1 Billion. You Flee to Florida. Then the Tax Man Knocks." Institutional Investor, June 13, 2018, https://www.institutionalinvestor.com/article/b18ml4mx51k3kx/you-make-1-billion-you-flee-to-florida-then-the-tax-man-knocks

     Sam Roberts, "William E. Macaulay, 74, Booster of Tuition-Free Education, Dies," The New York Times, December 5, 2019, https://www.nytimes.com/2019/12/05/education/william-e-macaulay-dead.html

61   Forbes Billionaires Profiles, "#875 — C. Dean Metropoulos," Forbes Magazine, last updated November 12, 2020, https://www.forbes.com/profile/c-dean-metropoulos/?list=billionaires&sh=20fd369f7f46

     Forbes Billionaires Profiles, "#108 — Paul Tudor Jones, II.," Forbes Magazine, last updated November 12, 2020, https://www.forbes.com/profile/paul-tudor-jones-ii/?sh=52556e90719c

     Forbes Billionaires Profiles, "#2057 — Edward Lampert," Forbes Magazine, last updated November 12, 2020, https://www.forbes.com/profile/edward-lampert/?sh=2f5ee5c546d3

     Forbes Billionaires Profiles, "#26 — Thomas Peterffy," Forbes Magazine, last updated November 12, 2020, https://www.forbes.com/profile/thomas-peterffy/?sh=9664cc01c0f7

62   Christopher Keating, "Income Tax Revenue Decline Expected To Hit $1.46 Billion By 2018," Hartford Courant, May 1, 2017, http://www.courant.com/politics/hc-consensus-revenue-update-20170501-story.html

63   Connecticut By The Numbers, "CT Aims to Keep Ultra-Wealthy in State; Tracks Tax Payments of Top 100 Earners," CTbythenumbers.com, May 5, 2016, https://ctbythenumbers.news/ctnews/2016/05/05/ct-aims-to-keep-ultra-wealthy-in-state-tracks-tax-payments-of-top-100-earners

64   Michelle Celarier, "You Make $1 Billion. You Flee to Florida. Then the Tax Man Knocks." Institutional Investor, June 13, 2018, https://www.institutionalinvestor.com/article/b18ml4mx51k3kx/you-make-1-billion-you-flee-to-florida-then-the-tax-man-knocks

65   Office of the State Comptroller, "Comptroller Lembo Says State On Track To End Fiscal Year 2017 With $107.2-Million Deficit," State of Connecticut, July 3, 2017, http://www.osc.ct.gov/public/news/releases/20170703.html

66  Janelle Camenga, "Does Your State Have an Estate or Inheritance Tax?" Tax Foundation, September 2, 2020, https://taxfoundation.org/state-estate-tax-state-inheritance-tax-2020/

Scott Drenkard & Richard Borean, "Does Your State Have an Estate or Inheritance Tax?" Tax Foundation, May 5, 2015, https://taxfoundation.org/does-your-state-have-estate-or-inheritance-tax/

67  Morgan Scarboro, "Does Your State Have an Estate or Inheritance Tax?" Tax Foundation, May 25, 2017, https://taxfoundation.org/state-estate-inheritance-tax/

68  Suzanne Bates, "A Better Place to Die: Reforming Connecticut's Estate Tax," Yankee Institute for Public Policy, Jan. 22, 2016, http://www.yankeeinstitute.org/policy-briefs/a-better-place-to-die-reforming-connecticuts-estate-tax/.

69  Ibid.

70  Connecticut General Assembly Office of Legislative Research, "Estate, Inheritance, and Gift Taxes in CT and Other States," State of Connecticut, September 2, 2020, https://www.cga.ct.gov/2020/rpt/pdf/2020-R-0180.pdf

71  Department of Revenue Services, "Estate Tax Study," Connecticut Office of Policy and Management, *State of Connecticut*, February 1, 2008, https://portal.ct.gov/-/media/DRS/Research/EstateTaxStudy/EstateTaxStudyFinalReportpdf.pdf

72  Ibid.

73  Ibid.

74  David DeLucia, "Goodbye Connecticut — Darien Resident Says Gift Tax Forcing Him To Leave," Hartford Courant, March 31, 2017, http://www.courant.com/opinion/insight/hc-op-insight-delucia-leaving-ct--20170401-story.html

75  Richard Rubin, "Wealthy avoid taxes by moving assets to no-tax states," Bloomberg News, Dec. 29, 2013, https://www.bloomberg.com/news/articles/2013-12-18/wealthy-n-y-residents-escape-tax-with-trusts-in-nevada

76  Connecticut Department of Revenue Services, "Department of Revenue Services Annual Reports," State of Connecticut, 2020, https://portal.ct.gov/DRS/DRS-Reports/Annual-Reports/Department-of-Revenue-Services-Annual-Reports

77  "Massachusetts Lawmakers Pass Bill to Raise Income and Gas Taxes," The New York Times, July 8, 1990, http://www.nytimes.com/1990/07/08/us/massachusetts-lawmakers-pass-bill-to-raise-income-and-gas-taxes.html

78  Katherine Loughead, "State Individual Income Tax Rates and Brackets for 2020," Tax Foundation, February 4, 2020, https://taxfoundation.org/state-individual-income-tax-rates-and-brackets-for-2020/

79  Dan Ring, "Gov. Deval Patrick calls for increase in Massachusetts' income tax, cut in sales tax," The Springfield Republican, Jan. 13, 2016, http://www.masslive.com/politics/index.ssf/2013/01/deval_patrick_calls_for_cut_in.html

80  OpenDOR, "Corporate tax rate drops to 8.0 percent effective January 1," Massachusetts Department of Revenue, *Commonwealth of Massachusetts*, Dec. 30, 2011, https://blog.mass.gov/revenue/current-affairs-2/corporate-tax-rate-drops-to-

80-percent-effective-january-1/

81  Fox, Justin. "The Massachusetts Tax-Cut Miracle," Bloomberg News, July 25, 2017. https://www.bloomberg.com/view/articles/2017-07-25/the-massachusetts-tax-cut-miracle.

82  Jared Walczak & Janelle Cammenga, "2021 State Business Tax Climate Index," Tax Foundation, October 21, 2020, https://taxfoundation.org/2021-state-business-tax-climate-index/

83  Federal Reserve Economic Database, "Per Capita Personal Income in Massachusetts (MAPCPI)," Federal Reserve Bank of St. Louis, last updated September 24, 2020, https://fred.stlouisfed.org/series/MAPCPI

84  Federal Reserve Economic Database, "All Employees: Total Nonfarm in Massachusetts (MANA)," Federal Reserve Bank of St. Louis, last updated October 20, 2020, https://fred.stlouisfed.org/series/MANA

85  Federal Reserve Economic Database, "Unemployment Rate in Massachusetts (MAUR)," Federal Reserve Bank of St. Louis, last updated June 24, 2020, https://fred.stlouisfed.org/series/MAUR

86  Phoenix Wealth & Affluent Monitor, "Report: Millionaire Rankings by State — Through Year-End 2019," Phoenix Marketing International, 2020, https://www.phoenixmi.com/learn/report-millionaire-rankings-by-state-through-year-end-2019/

87  Christopher Keating, "GE, Aetna, Travelers Criticize State Tax Increases," Hartford Courant, June 2, 2015, http://www.courant.com/politics/capitol-watch/hc-lawmakers-debate-revenue-estimates-liquor-changes-20150601-story.html

88  Rich Scinto, "Several New Taxes Proposed For Connecticut," New Canaan Patch, April 21, 2017, https://patch.com/connecticut/newcanaan/several-new-taxes-proposed-connecticut

89  Christopher Keating, "Malloy And GOP Say Hedge Fund Tax Could Drive Wealthy Out," Hartford Courant, April 11, 2017, http://www.courant.com/politics/hc-taxes-on-hedge-funds-20170411-story.html

90  Michael P. Norton, "Proposed 'Millionaire's Tax' May Push Wealthy To Move Out Of Mass., New Analysis Finds," WBUR News, June 12, 2017, https://www.wbur.org/news/2017/06/12/millionaires-tax-effect-wealthy-report

91  California Secretary of State, "Text of Proposed Laws," State of California, 2012, https://vig.cdn.sos.ca.gov/2012/general/pdf/text-proposed-laws-v2.pdf#nameddest=prop30

92  Ibid.

93  Xavier Giroud & Josh Rauh, "State Taxation and the Reallocation of Business Activity: Evidence from Establishment-Level Data," The University of Chicago Press, April 9, 2019, https://www.journals.uchicago.edu/doi/pdf/10.1086/701357

94  Dale Kasler, "A tax cut for Californians? Yes, really," The Sacramento Bee, December 30, 2016, https://www.sacbee.com/news/business/article123813839.html

95  California Department of Education, "Proposition 30 Impact to State Aid," State of California, last updated February 18, 2020, https://www.cde.ca.gov/fg/aa/pa/prop30impact12p1.asp

Public Policy Institute of California, "Proposition 30 Archives," 2020, https://www.ppic.org/blog/tag/proposition-30/

96  Joshua Rauh & Ryan J. Shyu, "Behavioral Responses to State Income Taxation of High Earners: Evidence from California," National Bureau of Economic Research, October 2019, https://www.nber.org/papers/w26349

97  Joshua Rauh & Ryan J. Shyu, "Behavioral Responses to State Income Taxation of High Earners: Evidence from California," National Bureau of Economic Research, October 2019, https://www.nber.org/papers/w26349

98  Joshua Rauh & Ryan J. Shyu, "Behavioral Responses to State Income Taxation of High Earners: Evidence from California," National Bureau of Economic Research, October 2019, https://www.nber.org/papers/w26349

99  Derek Miller, "States With the Most Million-Dollar Earners," Smart Asset, February 14, 2018, https://smartasset.com/taxes/states-with-the-most-million-dollar-earners

100 Morgan Scarboro, "State Individual Income Tax Rates and Brackets for 2018," Tax Foundation, March 5, 2018, https://taxfoundation.org/state-individual-income-tax-rates-brackets-2018/

Michael Walker, "CA IRS State-to-State Migration," Data Made Useful, 2020, https://public.tableau.com/profile/michael.walker#!/vizhome/CA_IRS_StatetoState_Migration/YearlyAGIFlow

101 Joshua Rauh & Ryan J. Shyu, "Behavioral Responses to State Income Taxation of High Earners: Evidence from California," National Bureau of Economic Research, October 2019, https://www.nber.org/papers/w26349

102 Tax Policy Center Briefing Book, "How did the TCJA change the standard and itemized deductions?" Tax Policy Center, 2018, https://www.taxpolicycenter.org/briefing-book/how-did-tcja-change-standard-deduction-and-itemized-deductions

103 Sarah Mervosh & Jill Cowan, "'Welcome to Texas!': Musk's California Departure Stokes the States' Rivalry," The New York Times, December 9, 2020, https://www.nytimes.com/2020/12/09/us/elon-musk-texas-california.html

104 Robert Frank, "Elon Musk could save billions in taxes if Tesla moves its headquarters to Nevada or Texas," CNBC LLC., last updated May 12, 2020, https://www.cnbc.com/2020/05/11/elon-musk-could-save-billions-in-taxes-if-tesla-moves-its-headquarters.html

Nirah Chokshi, "Tesla to Move Its Headquarters to Austin, Texas, in Blow to California," The New York Times, last updated October 13, 2021, https://www.nytimes.com/2021/10/07/business/tesla-texas-headquarters.html

105 2021 State Business Tax Climate Index, "Corporate Taxes," Tax Foundation, 2020, https://statetaxindex.org/tax/corporate/

106 William Ruger & Jason Sorens, "Freedom in the 50 States," Cato Institute, 2020, https://www.freedominthe50states.org/regulatory

107 Claire Kalia, "What is a Sole Proprietorship?" Kalia Law P.C., May 13, 2014, https://www.kalialawpc.com/2014/05/13/what-is-a-sole-proprietorship/

108 United States Small Business Administration, "Small Business Profile: California," 2014, https://www.sba.gov/sites/default/files/files/California13(1).pdf

109 California Chamber of Commerce, "CalChamber Board Takes Positions on Proposed Initiatives," May 23, 2016, https://advocacy.calchamber.com/2016/05/23/calchamber-board-takes-positions-on-proposed-initiatives/

110 Allen Young, "Why big business laid down on Prop 55," Sacramento Business Journal, October 14, 2016, https://www.bizjournals.com/sacramento/news/2016/10/14/why-big-business-laid-down-on-prop-55.html

111 Ibid.

112 Ballotpedia, "California Proposition 55, Extension of the Proposition 30 Income Tax Increase (2016)," 2016, https://ballotpedia.org/California_Proposition_55,_Extension_of_the_Proposition_30_Income_Tax_Increase_(2016)

Ballotpedia, "California Proposition 30, Sales and Income Tax Increase (2012)," 2012, https://ballotpedia.org/California_Proposition_30,_Sales_and_Income_Tax_Increase_(2012)

113 Joseph Vranich & Lee E. Ohanian, "Why Company Headquarters are Leaving California in Unprecedented Numbers," The Hoover Institution, August 2021, https://www.hoover.org/sites/default/files/research/docs/21117-ohanian-vranich-3.pdf

114 Joshua Rauh & Ryan J. Shyu, "Behavioral Responses to State Income Taxation of High Earners: Evidence from California," National Bureau of Economic Research, October 2019, https://www.nber.org/papers/w26349

115 Ibid.

116 Ibid.

117 California Legislative Analyst's Office, "Hearing Concerning Propositions 30, 31, and 38," State of California, September 24, 2012, https://lao.ca.gov/handouts/state_admin/2012/Propositions_30_31_38_Sept_24_12.pdf

California State Controller, "California Department of Education Audit Report of Education Protection Account Recorded In The State General Fund — July 1, 2012, through June 30, 2015," State of California, August 2016, https://trackprop55.sco.ca.gov/AuditReport/CDE_EPA_AuditReport2012to2015.pdf

118 Mary Murphy, Akshay Iyengar, & Alexandria Zhang, "Tax Revenue Volatility Varies Across States, Revenue Streams," Pew Research Center, August 29, 2018, https://www.pewtrusts.org/en/research-and-analysis/articles/2018/08/29/tax-revenue-volatility-varies-across-states-revenue-streams

119 California Department of Finance, "Governor's Budget Summary — 2019–2020 — Revenue Estimates," State of California, January 10, 2020, http://ebudget.ca.gov/

2019-20/pdf/BudgetSummary/RevenueEstimates.pdf

120 California Department of Finance, "General Fund Revenue Forecast Reconciliation with the 2008–09 May Revision," State of California, 2008, http://www.ebudget.ca.gov/2008-09-EN/Enacted/BudgetSummary/ImagePages/FG-REV-01.html

121 Ashlea Ebeling, "Arizona Voters Approve Massive Tax Hike On High Earners, Could Your State Be Next?" Forbes Magazine, November 4, 2020, Massive https://www.forbes.com/sites/ashleaebeling/2020/11/04/arizona-voters-approve-massive-tax-hike-on-high-earners-could-your-state-be-next/?sh=175a0ff1f98f

122 Mary Murphy, Akshay Iyengar, & Alexandria Zhang, "Tax Revenue Volatility Varies Across States, Revenue Streams," Pew Research Center, August 29, 2018, https://www.pewtrusts.org/en/research-and-analysis/articles/2018/08/29/tax-revenue-volatility-varies-across-states-revenue-streams

123 Ballotpedia, "Massachusetts Graduated Income Tax, Question 1 (1962)," December 23, 2013, https://ballotpedia.org/Massachusetts_Graduated_Income_Tax,_Question_1_(1962)

Ballotpedia, "Massachusetts Graduated Income Tax, Question 2 (1968)," December 23, 2013, https://ballotpedia.org/Massachusetts_Graduated_Income_Tax,_Question_2_(1968)

Ballotpedia, "Massachusetts Graduated Income Tax Based on Federal Income Tax, Question 6 (1972)," December 23, 2013, https://ballotpedia.org/Massachusetts_Graduated_Income_Tax_Based_on_Federal_Income_Tax,_Question_6_(1972)

Ballotpedia, "Massachusetts Graduated Income Tax, Question 2 (1976)," December 23, 2013, https://ballotpedia.org/Massachusetts_Graduated_Income_Tax,_Question_2_(1976)

Ballotpedia, "Massachusetts Graduated Income Tax Amendment, Question 6 (1994)," https://ballotpedia.org/Massachusetts_Graduated_Income_Tax_Amendment,_Question_6_(1994)

124 Joseph Bishop-Henchman, "Massachusetts May Set Its Income Tax Rate In The Constitution. How Unusual Is That?" Tax Foundation, February 2, 2016, https://taxfoundation.org/massachusetts-may-set-its-income-tax-rate-constitution-how-unusual/

125 Raise Up Massachusetts, "Fair Share Amendment," https://www.raiseupma.org/fair-share-amendment-2022/

126 Massachusetts Executive Office of Administration and Finance, "FY2020 Budget Summary," Commonwealth of Massachusetts, July 31, 2019, https://budget.digital.mass.gov/summary/fy20/enacted

127 Brief of the Attorney General, in *Anderson v. Healey,* 579 Mass. 780 (2018), available at http://masscases.com/briefs/sjc/479/479mass780/SJC-12422_03_Appellee_Attorney_General_Brief.pdf

128 Massachusetts Supreme Judicial Court, "SJC 12422," Commonwealth of Massachusetts, December 9, 2020, https://www.youtube.com/watch?v=O8bFdcNvQKQ&feature=youtu.be

129 Proposition 30 also included a temporary increase in the state sales tax from 7.25% to 7.5% for four years.

130 Ballotpedia, "California Proposition 30, Sales and Income Tax Increase (2012)," 2012, https://ballotpedia.org/California_Proposition_30,_Sales_and_Income_Tax_Increase_(2012)

131 Ballotpedia, "California Proposition 55, Extension of the Proposition 30 Income Tax Increase (2016)," 2016, https://ballotpedia.org/California_Proposition_55,_Extension_of_the_Proposition_30_Income_Tax_Increase_(2016)

132 Kenneth Kapphahn, "The 2021–2022 Budget: The Fiscal Outlook for Schools and Community Colleges," California Legislative Analyst's Office, November 18, 2020, https://lao.ca.gov/Publications/Report/4298

133 Adventures in Ed Funding, "Have We Got A Proposition For You? Proposition 98 and a Brisk Hike Through California School Funding History," CASBO, 2020, https://www.buzzsprout.com/847942/2777395

134 California Secretary of State, "Prop 30: Temporary Taxes To Fund Education. Guaranteed Local Public Safety Funding. Initiative Constitutional Amendment." State of California, 2012, http://vigarchive.sos.ca.gov/2012/general/propositions/30/arguments-rebuttals.htm

135 Document provided by California Legislative Analyst's Office; California Comprehensive Annual Financial Report for Fiscal Years ended June 30, 2013 to 2019, https://www.sco.ca.gov/ard_state_cafr.html, Legislative Analyst's Office, 2020–21 Budget Overview of the California Spending Plan (Final Version); https://lao.ca.gov/Publications/Report/4263; Governor's Budget Summary, Summary Charts, 2020–21 http://www.ebudget.ca.gov/2020–21/pdf/BudgetSummary/SummaryCharts.pdf., California Legislative Analyst's Office Reports 4174, 3930, 3355, and 3526, https://lao.ca.gov/Publications; Analysis by Pioneer Institute.

136 Kenneth Kapphahn, "Proposition 98 Outlook," California Legislative Analyst's Office, November 14, 2018, https://lao.ca.gov/Publications/Report/3897

Kenneth Kapphahn, Ryan Anderson, & Amy Li, "Proposition 98 Analysis," California Legislative Analyst's Office, February 13, 2019, https://lao.ca.gov/Publications/Report/3930#Minimum_Guarantee

137 Document provided by California Legislative Analyst's Office; California Comprehensive Annual Financial Report for Fiscal Years ended June 30, 2013 to 2019, https://www.sco.ca.gov/ard_state_cafr.html, Legislative Analyst's Office, 2020–21 Budget Overview of the California Spending Plan (Final Version) https://lao.ca.gov/Publications/Report/4263; Analysis by Pioneer Institute.

138 California Department of Education Audit Report — Education Protection Account recorded in the state general fund, July 1, 2012, through June 30, 2015, https://trackprop55.sco.ca.gov/AuditReport/CDE_EPA_AuditReport2012to2015.pdf; California Department of Education Audit Report — Education Protection Account recorded in the state general fund, July 1, 2015, through June 30, 2017, https://trackprop55.sco.ca.gov/AuditReport/CDE_EPA_AuditReport_FY2015-17.pdf; Department Detail of Appropriation and Adjustments, California

State Budget 2019–20, http://www.ebudget.ca.gov/2019-20/pdf/Enacted/GovernorsBudget/6000/6100RWA.pdf; Department Detail of Appropriation and Adjustments, California State Budget 2020–21, http://www.ebudget.ca.gov/2020-21/pdf/Enacted/GovernorsBudget/6000/6100FCS.pdf. Analysis by Pioneer Institute.

139 U.S. Bureau of Labor Statistics, "Quarterly Census of Employment and Wages," U.S. Department of Labor, last updated September 23, 2020, https://www.bls.gov/cew/downloadable-data-files.htm

140 BLS Quarterly Census of Employment and Wages (QCEW) quarterly data files 2013–20. Pioneer Institute analysis.

141 Ibid.

142 BLS Quarterly Census of Employment and Wages (QCEW) quarterly data files 2013–20. Pioneer Institute analysis.

143 National Education Association. Rankings and Estimates Rankings of the States 2013 and 2019. Pioneer Institute analysis.

144 National Education Association, "Rankings of the States 2014 and Estimates of School Statistics 2015," March 2015, https://www.nea.org/sites/default/files/2020-07/NEA_Rankings_And_Estimates-2015-03-11a.pdf

National Education Association, "Rankings of the States 2019 and Estimates of School Statistics 2020," June 2020, https://www.nea.org/sites/default/files/2020-07/2020%20Rankings%20and%20Estimates%20Report%20FINAL_0.pdf

145 California State Controller, "Government Compensation in California," State of California, 2021, https://publicpay.ca.gov

146 National Education Association. Rankings and Estimates Rankings of the States 2013 and 2019. Pioneer Institute analysis.

147 California State Controller – Government Compensation in California https://publicpay.ca.gov. Pioneer Institute analysis.

148 Raise Up Massachusetts, "Fair Share Amendment," https://www.raiseupma.org/fair-share-amendment-2022/

149 Massachusetts Supreme Judicial Court, "579 Mass. 780 Anderson v. Attorney General," Commonwealth of Massachusetts, 2018 Appellee Brief — Attorney General. http://masscases.com/briefs/sjc/479/479mass780/SJC-12422_03_Appellee_Attorney_General_Brief.pdf

150 U.S. Bureau of Labor Statistics, "Quarterly Census of Employment and Wages," U.S. Department of Labor, last updated September 23, 2020, https://www.bls.gov/cew/downloadable-data-files.htm

151 "Civilian Unemployment Rate," U.S. Bureau of Labor Statistics (U.S. Bureau of Labor Statistics), accessed February 8, 2021, https://www.bls.gov/charts/employment-situation/civilian-unemployment-rate.htm

152 Robin Foster and E.J. Mundell, "House Passes $3 Trillion Coronavirus Stimulus Package," U.S. News & World Report (U.S. News & World Report, May 16, 2020),

https://www.usnews.com/news/health-news/articles/2020-05-16/house-passes-3-trillion-coronavirus-stimulus-package

153 "Civilian Unemployment Rate," U.S. Bureau of Labor Statistics (U.S. Bureau of Labor Statistics, January 2021), https://www.bls.gov/charts/employment-situation/civilian-unemployment-rate.htm

154 "How Many Employees Work for the Commonwealth? For Individual Departments?," Comptroller of the Commonwealth (Commonwealth of Massachusetts, January 25, 2021), https://massfinance.state.ma.us/CommonCents/commonEmployeeResult_new.asp?pg=6&cat=employee&num=1

"Databases, Tables & Calculators by Subject," U.S. Bureau of Labor Statistics (U.S. Bureau of Labor Statistics), accessed February 8, 2021, https://data.bls.gov/timeseries/LASST250000000000005?amp%253bdata_tool=XGtable&output_view=data&include_graphs=true

155 "How Many Employees Work for the Commonwealth? For Individual Departments?," Comptroller of the Commonwealth (Commonwealth of Massachusetts, January 25, 2021), https://massfinance.state.ma.us/CommonCents/commonEmployeeResult_new.asp?pg=6&cat=employee&num=1

156 "Unemployment Rate 16.1 Percent in Massachusetts, 4.5 Percent in Utah, in July 2020," U.S. Bureau of Labor Statistics (U.S. Bureau of Labor Statistics, August 27, 2020), https://www.bls.gov/opub/ted/2020/unemployment-rate-16-point-1-percent-in-massachusetts-4-point-5-percent-in-utah-in-july-2020.htm

157 "Databases, Tables & Calculators by Subject," U.S. Bureau of Labor Statistics (U.S. Bureau of Labor Statistics), accessed February 8, 2021, https://data.bls.gov/timeseries/LASST250000000000005?amp%253bdata_tool=XGtable&output_view=data&include_graphs=true

158 Ibid.

159 Ibid.

160 Ibid.

161 Ibid.

162 "How Many Employees Work for the Commonwealth? For Individual Departments?," Comptroller of the Commonwealth (Commonwealth of Massachusetts, January 25, 2021), https://massfinance.state.ma.us/CommonCents/commonEmployeeResult_new.asp?pg=6&cat=employee&num=1

163 "Databases, Tables & Calculators by Subject," U.S. Bureau of Labor Statistics (U.S. Bureau of Labor Statistics), accessed February 8, 2021, https://data.bls.gov/timeseries/LASST250000000000005?amp%253bdata_tool=XGtable&output_view=data&include_graphs=true

164 Ibid.

165 "How Many Employees Work for the Commonwealth? For Individual Departments?," Comptroller of the Commonwealth (Commonwealth of Massachusetts, January 25, 2021), https://massfinance.state.ma.us/CommonCents/commonEmployeeResult_new.asp?pg=6&cat=employee&num=1

166 "Massachusetts," U.S. Bureau of Labor Statistics (U.S. Bureau of Labor Statistics), accessed February 8, 2021, https://www.bls.gov/regions/new-england/massachusetts.htm#eag

167 "How Many Employees Work for the Commonwealth? For Individual Departments?," Comptroller of the Commonwealth (Commonwealth of Massachusetts, January 25, 2021), https://massfinance.state.ma.us/CommonCents/commonEmployeeResult_new.asp?pg=6&cat=employee&num=1

168 Calculated using total "employment" numbers provided by the Bureau of Labor Statistics and total state employment numbers provided by the Comptroller of the Commonwealth

169 "Percent Change in Number of Small Businesses Open, Massachusetts," Economic Tracker (Opportunity Insights, January 27, 2021), https://tracktherecovery.org/

170 Kyle Pomerleau, "The High Burden of State and Federal Capital Gains Tax Rates in the United States," Tax Foundation, March 24, 2015, https://taxfoundation.org/high-burden-state-and-federal-capital-gains-tax-rates-united-states/

171 William McBride, "What Is the Evidence on Taxes and Growth?" Tax Foundation, December 18, 2012, https://taxfoundation.org/what-evidence-taxes-and-growth/

Scott A. Hodge & Brian Hickman, "How Lower Corporate Tax Rates Lead to Higher Worker Wages," Tax Foundation, 2018, https://files.taxfoundation.org/20190516115624/How-Lower-Corporate-Tax-Rates-Lead-to-Higher-Worker-Wages.pdf

172 Capital Flows, "The Cost of Increasing Tax Rates On Capital Gains and Dividends," Forbes Magazine, April 5, 2012, https://www.forbes.com/sites/realspin/2012/04/05/the-cost-of-increasing-tax-rates-on-capital-gains-and-dividends/?sh=3e6957424f06#f

173 Kyle Pomerleau, "The High Burden of State and Federal Capital Gains Tax Rates in the United States," Tax Foundation, March 24, 2015, https://taxfoundation.org/high-burden-state-and-federal-capital-gains-tax-rates-united-states/

174 GreenTraderTax, "Best, Worst & The Decent Tax States For Traders (Recording)," Green & Company, Inc., August 2, 2016, https://greentradertax.com/events/tax-battle-of-the-states/

Tax Policy Center, "State Treatment of Capital Gains and Losses," Urban Institute & Brookings Institution, March 13, 2020, https://www.taxpolicycenter.org/statistics/state-treatment-capital-gains-and-losses

175 Michael Walker, "Individual Tax Returns — All States," Data Made Useful, 2021, https://irsdatadiscovery.com/individual-tax-returns-all-states

176 Massachusetts Technology Collaborative, "The Annual Index of the Massachusetts Innovation Economy (2019 Edition)," State Library of Massachusetts, August 31, 2020, https://archives.lib.state.ma.us/handle/2452/832518

177 Ibid.

178 Sloan Management Review, "The Multiplier Effect of Innovation Jobs,"

Massachusetts Institute of Technology, June 6, 2012, https://sloanreview.mit.edu/article/the-multiplier-effect-of-innovation-jobs/

179 Michael Walker, "Individual Tax Returns — All States," Data Made Useful, 2021, https://irsdatadiscovery.com/individual-tax-returns-all-states

180 MassEconomix, "Employment by Industry," Pioneer Institute for Public Policy Research, 2021, https://masseconomix.org/industry/employment-by-industry

181 Ernst and Young, "Large S Corporations and the Tax Cuts and Jobs Act," S Corporation Association, October 2019, https://s-corp.org/wp-content/uploads/2019/10/EY-S-Corporation-Association-report-Economic-footprint-and-impact-of-TCJA-on-large-S-corporations-October-2019.pdf

182 Aaron Krupkin and Adam Looney, "9 facts about pass-through businesses," The Brookings Institution, May 15, 2017, https://www.brookings.edu/research/9-facts-about-pass-through-businesses/

183 Julia Kagan, "C Corporation," Investopedia, October 20, 2020, https://www.investopedia.com/terms/c/c-corporation.asp

184 Grant Thornton, "Should pass-through owners switch to C-corp status," May 27, 2019, https://www.grantthornton.com/library/articles/tax/2018/switch-C-corp-status.aspx

185 U.S. Census Bureau, County Business Patterns, by Legal Form of Organization and Employment for the U.S., States, and Selected Geographies: 2019. Analysis by Pioneer Institute. https://data.census.gov/cedsci/table?q=CBP2019.CB1900CBP&g=0400000US25&d=ECNSVY%20Business%20Patterns%20County%20Business%20Patterns&tid=CBP2019.CB1900CBP&hidePreview=true

186 Ernst and Young, "Large S Corporations and the Tax Cuts and Jobs Act," S Corporation Association, October 2019, https://s-corp.org/wp-content/uploads/2019/10/EY-S-Corporation-Association-report-Economic-footprint-and-impact-of-TCJA-on-large-S-corporations-October-2019.pdf

Aaron Krupkin and Adam Looney, "9 facts about pass-through businesses," The Brookings Institution, May 15, 2017, https://www.brookings.edu/research/9-facts-about-pass-through-businesses/

187 "Overview of Entity Classification," Internal Revenue Service, September 24, 2017, https://www.irs.gov/pub/int_practice_units/ore_c_19_02_01.pdf

188 Janette Wilson & Pearson Liddell, "Sales of Capital Assets Data Reported on Individual Tax Returns, 2007–2012," Internal Revenue Service, Winter 2016, https://www.irs.gov/pub/irs-soi/soi-a-inca-id1604.pdf

189 Ibid.

190 IRS 2010–2018 SOI Tax Stats Historic Table 2 Individual Income and Tax Data, by State and Size of Adjusted Gross Income. Analysis by Pioneer Institute

191 IRS 2010–2018 SOI Tax Stats Historic Table 2 Individual Income and Tax Data, by State and Size of Adjusted Gross Income. Analysis by Pioneer Institute

192 Robert Carroll, Douglas Holtz-Eakin, Mark Rider, and Harvey S. Rosen, "Personal Income Taxes and the Growth of Small Firms," National Bureau of Economic Research, Working Paper 7980, October 2000, https://www.nber.org/system/files/working_papers/w7980/w7980.pdf

193 Mina Baliamoune-Lutz and Pierre Garello. "Tax Structure and Entrepreneurship." *Small Business Economics* 42, no. 1, 2014. http://www.jstor.org/stable/43553726

194 Keith M Phaneuf, "Business groups hope to sink tax hike on pass-through entities," the CT Mirror, May 31, 2019, https://ctmirror.org/2019/05/31/business-groups-hope-to-sink-tax-hike-on-pass-through-entities/

195 Ibid.

196 Ibid.

197 Darla Mercado, "Taxes are about to rise for New Jersey millionaires. There aren't many ways to duck the levies," CNBC, September 24, 2020, https://www.cnbc.com/2020/09/24/taxes-are-about-to-rise-for-new-jersey-millionaires.html

198 Nicholas Pugliese, "NJ millionaires tax: Here are the arguments for and against the controversial increase," northjersey.com, April 17, 2019, https://www.northjersey.com/story/news/new-jersey/2019/04/17/nj-taxes-millionaires-tax-debate-larger-political-fight-murphy-sweeney/3483726002/

199 Janelle Cammenga, "Seventh Time's the Charm: New Jersey Passes Millionaire's Tax," Tax Foundation, September 30, 2020, https://taxfoundation.org/new-jersey-millionaires-tax-fy-2021/

200 Rebekah Paxton, Andrew Mikula, and Greg Sullivan, "Public Policy Guide for Economic Recovery From Covid-19 for Hospitality and Retail Businesses," Pioneer Institute, July 29, 2020, https://pioneerinstitute.org/pioneer-research/covid-pioneer-research/public-policy-guide-for-economic-recovery-from-covid-19-in-the-retail-and-hospitality-sectors/

201 Vik Krishnan, Ryan Mann, Nathan Seitzman, and Nina Wittkamp, "Hospitality and Covid-19: How long until 'no vacancy' for US hotels?," McKinsey & Company, June 2020, https://www.mckinsey.com/industries/travel-logistics-and-transport-infrastructure/our-insights/hospitality-and-covid-19-how-long-until-no-vacancy-for-us-hotels#

202 Ibid.

203 Massachusetts Department of Revenue, email message to Pioneer Institute, February 24, 2021.

204 https://ballotpedia.org/Massachusetts_Income_Tax_for_Education_and_Transportation_Amendment_(2022)

205 U.S. Census Bureau, County Business Patterns, by Legal Form of Organization and Employment for the U.S., States, and Selected Geographies: 2019. Analysis by Pioneer Institute. https://data.census.gov/cedsci/table?q=CBP2019.CB1900CBP&g=0400000US25&d=ECNSVY%20Business%20Patterns%20County%20Business%20Patterns&tid=CBP2019.CB1900CBP&hidePreview=true

206 Ibid.

207 United States Internal Revenue Service, "Individual Income and Tax Data, by State and Size of Adjusted Gross Income, Tax Year 2018 (Massachusetts)," U.S. Department of the Treasury, last updated May 24, 2021, https://www.irs.gov/statistics/soi-tax-stats-historic-table-2

208 U.S. Census Bureau County Business Patterns, including ZIP Code Business Patterns, by Legal Form of Organization and Employment Size Class for the U.S., States, and Selected Geographies: 2019 https://data.census.gov/cedsci/table?q=CBP2019.CB1900CBP&g=0400000US25&d=ECNSVY%20Business%20Patterns%20County%20Business%20Patterns&tid=CBP2019.CB1900CBP&hidePreview=true

209 Michael Lucci, "Reforming Massachusetts Corporate Excise Tax for S Corporations," Tax Foundation, January 21, 2020, https://taxfoundation.org/massachusetts-corporate-excise-tax-s-corporations

210 Jeff Brown, "Beware of Phantom Income and the Tax It Brings," U.S. News and World Report, July 9, 2018, https://money.usnews.com/investing/investing-101/articles/2018-07-09/beware-of-phantom-income-and-the-tax-it-brings

211 Greg Ryan, "Millionaire's tax or business tax? Businesses say proposal may hurt growth in Massachusetts," Boston Business Journal, last updated April 14, 2017, https://www.bizjournals.com/boston/news/2017/04/14/millionaire-s-tax-or-business-tax-businesses-say.html

212 Ibid.

213 Dan Ring, "Gov. Deval Patrick calls for increase in Massachusetts' income tax, cut in sales tax," The Springfield Republican, last updated January 7, 2019, https://www.masslive.com/politics/2013/01/deval_patrick_calls_for_cut_in.html

214 William McBride, "What Is the Evidence on Taxes and Growth?" Tax Foundation, December 18, 2012, https://taxfoundation.org/what-evidence-taxes-and-growth/
Scott A. Hodge & Brian Hickman, "How Lower Corporate Tax Rates Lead to Higher Worker Wages," Tax Foundation, 2018, https://files.taxfoundation.org/20190516115624/How-Lower-Corporate-Tax-Rates-Lead-to-Higher-Worker-Wages.pdf

215 Capital Flows, "The Cost of Increasing Tax Rates On Capital Gains and Dividends," Forbes Magazine, April 5, 2012, https://www.forbes.com/sites/realspin/2012/04/05/the-cost-of-increasing-tax-rates-on-capital-gains-and-dividends/?sh=3e6957424f06#f

216 Janette Wilson & Pearson Liddell, "Sales of Capital Assets Data Reported on Individual Tax Returns, 2007–2012," Internal Revenue Service, Winter 2016, https://www.irs.gov/pub/irs-soi/soi-a-inca-id1604.pdf

217 Ibid.

218 Zillow Research, "Housing Data," Zillow, Inc., 2021, https://www.zillow.com/research/data/

US Inflation Calculator, "Consumer Price Index Data from 1913 to 2021," CoinNews Media Group LLC, 2021, https://www.usinflationcalculator.com/ inflation/consumer-price-index-and-annual-percent-changes-from-1913-to-2008/

219 Scott A. Hodge, "Who Are America's Millionaires?" Tax Foundation, June 15, 2012, https://taxfoundation.org/who-are-americas-millionaires/

220 Scott A. Hodge, "Who Are America's Millionaires?" Tax Foundation, June 15, 2012, https://taxfoundation.org/who-are-americas-millionaires/

221 Massachusetts Department of Revenue, email message to authors, February 24, 2021.

222 Massachusetts Department of Revenue, email message to authors, February 24, 2021.

223 Data Made Useful, "Gross Taxpayer Migration — All States," IRS Tax Data Discovery, 2020, https://irsdatadiscovery.com/gross-taxpayer-migration-all-states

224 Data Made Useful, "Gross Taxpayer Migration — All States," IRS Tax Data Discovery, 2020, https://irsdatadiscovery.com/gross-taxpayer-migration-all-states

225 Raise Up Massachusetts, "Fair Share Amendment," February 13, 2018, https:// raiseupma.org/campaigns/fair-share-amendment/

226 Massachusetts General Court, "Proposal for Constitutional Amendment S.16," Commonwealth of Massachusetts, https://malegislature.gov/Bills/191/S16/Senate/ Proposal%20for%20Constitutional%20Amendment/Text

227 United States Bureau of Labor Statistics, "Consumer Price Index: Design," United States Department of Labor, last updated November 24, 2020, https://www.bls.gov/ opub/hom/cpi/design.htm

United States Bureau of Labor Statistics, "Chapter 17. The Consumer Price Index," United States Department of Labor, last updated February 14, 2018, https://www. bls.gov/opub/hom/pdf/homch17.pdf

United States Bureau of Labor Statistics, "Consumer Price Index," United States Department of Labor, last updated November 24, 2020, https://www.bls.gov/opub/ hom/cpi/pdf/cpi.pdf

228 Bradford Tax Institute, "History of Federal Income Tax Rates: 1913–2021," 2021, https://bradfordtaxinstitute.com/Free_Resources/Federal-Income-Tax-Rates.aspx

229 Amir El-Sibaie, "2021 Tax Brackets," Tax Foundation, October 27, 2020, https:// taxfoundation.org/2021-tax-brackets/#brackets

230 Jeff Desjardins, "How Americans Make and Spend Their Money," Visual Capitalist, March 19, 2019, https://www.visualcapitalist.com/how-americans-make-spend-money/

231 Michael P. Norton, "Lawmakers getting $4,258 hike in base pay," Commonwealth Magazine, January 1, 2021, https://commonwealthmagazine.org/state-government/ lawmakers-getting-4280-hike-in-base-pay/

232 Secretary of the Commonwealth of Massachusetts, "Statewide Ballot Questions —
Statistics by Year: 1919–2018," Commonwealth of Massachusetts, 2020,
https://www.sec.state.ma.us/ele/elebalm/balmresults.html#year1998

General Court of the Commonwealth of Massachusetts, "Proposal for
Constitutional Amendment H.86," Commonwealth of Massachusetts, 2021,
https://malegislature.gov/laws/constitution

Ballotpedia, "Massachusetts State Legislators Compensation Amendment,
Question 1 (1998)," https://ballotpedia.org/Massachusetts_State_Legislators_
Compensation_Amendment,_Question_1_(1998)

233 United States Bureau of Labor Statistics, "CPI for All Urban Consumers (CPI-U),"
United States Department of Labor, https://data.bls.gov/cgi-bin/surveymost?cu

Federal Reserve Economic Database, "Chained Consumer Price Index for All Urban
Consumers: All Items in U.S. City Average," last updated February 10, 2021, https://
fred.stlouisfed.org/series/SUUR0000SA0

U.S. Bureau of the Census, "Historical Income Tables: Households," United States
Department of Commerce, last updated September 8, 2020, https://www.census.
gov/data/tables/time-series/demo/income-poverty/historical-income-households.
html

U.S. Bureau of Economic Analysis, "Regional Data: GDP and Personal Income,"
United States Department of Commerce, https://apps.bea.gov/iTable/iTable.
cfm?acrdn=2&reqid=70&step=1#

234 United States Bureau of Labor Statistics, "CPI for All Urban Consumers (CPI-U),"
United States Department of Labor, https://data.bls.gov/cgi-bin/surveymost?cu

Federal Reserve Economic Database, "Chained Consumer Price Index for All Urban
Consumers: All Items in U.S. City Average," last updated February 10, 2021, https://
fred.stlouisfed.org/series/SUUR0000SA0

U.S. Bureau of the Census, "Historical Income Tables: Households," United States
Department of Commerce, last updated September 8, 2020, https://www.census.
gov/data/tables/time-series/demo/income-poverty/historical-income-households.
html

U.S. Bureau of Economic Analysis, "Regional Data: GDP and Personal Income,"
United States Department of Commerce, https://apps.bea.gov/iTable/iTable.
cfm?acrdn=2&reqid=70&step=1#

235 United States Bureau of Labor Statistics, "CPI for All Urban Consumers (CPI-U),"
United States Department of Labor, https://data.bls.gov/cgi-bin/surveymost?cu

Federal Reserve Economic Database, "Chained Consumer Price Index for All Urban
Consumers: All Items in U.S. City Average," last updated February 10, 2021, https://
fred.stlouisfed.org/series/SUUR0000SA0

U.S. Bureau of the Census, "Historical Income Tables: Households," United States
Department of Commerce, last updated September 8, 2020, https://www.census.
gov/data/tables/time-series/demo/income-poverty/historical-income-households.
html

U.S. Bureau of Economic Analysis, "Regional Data: GDP and Personal Income," United States Department of Commerce, https://apps.bea.gov/iTable/iTable. cfm?acrdn=2&reqid=70&step=1#

236 United States Bureau of Labor Statistics, "CPI for All Urban Consumers (CPI-U)," United States Department of Labor, https://data.bls.gov/cgi-bin/surveymost?cu

Federal Reserve Economic Database, "Chained Consumer Price Index for All Urban Consumers: All Items in U.S. City Average," last updated February 10, 2021, https://fred.stlouisfed.org/series/SUUR0000SA0

U.S. Bureau of the Census, "Historical Income Tables: Households," United States Department of Commerce, last updated September 8, 2020, https://www.census.gov/data/tables/time-series/demo/income-poverty/historical-income-households.html

237 United States Bureau of Labor Statistics, "CPI for All Urban Consumers (CPI-U)," United States Department of Labor, https://data.bls.gov/cgi-bin/surveymost?cu

Federal Reserve Economic Database, "Chained Consumer Price Index for All Urban Consumers: All Items in U.S. City Average," last updated February 10, 2021, https://fred.stlouisfed.org/series/SUUR0000SA0

U.S. Bureau of the Census, "Historical Income Tables: Households," United States Department of Commerce, last updated September 8, 2020, https://www.census.gov/data/tables/time-series/demo/income-poverty/historical-income-households.html

238 Federal Reserve Economic Database, "Chained Consumer Price Index for All Urban Consumers: All Items in U.S. City Average," last updated February 10, 2021, https://fred.stlouisfed.org/series/SUUR0000SA0

U.S. Bureau of the Census, "Historical Income Tables: Households," United States Department of Commerce, last updated September 8, 2020, https://www.census.gov/data/tables/time-series/demo/income-poverty/historical-income-households.html

239 Board of Governors of the Federal Reserve System, "Survey of Consumer Finances (SCF)," United States Federal Reserve Bank, last updated November 17, 2020, https://www.federalreserve.gov/econres/scfindex.htm

240 Massachusetts Budget and Policy Center, "Examining Tax Fairness," February 24, 2015, https://massbudget.org/reports/pdf/FactsAtAGlance_TaxFairness_UPDATE_1-16-2018.pdf

241 SEIU Local 888, "New Campaign for Increased Investment in Mass.," June 10, 2015, https://www.seiu888.org/2015/06/10/new-campaign-for-increased-investment-in-mass/

242 Massachusetts Budget and Policy Center, "Examining Tax Fairness," February 24, 2015, https://massbudget.org/reports/pdf/FactsAtAGlance_TaxFairness_UPDATE_1-16-2018.pdf

243 Liz Malm & Kyle Pomerleau, "Comments on Who Pays? A Distributional Analysis of the Tax Systems in All 50 States (Second Edition)," Tax Foundation, January 16,

2015, https://taxfoundation.org/comments-who-pays-distributional-analysis-tax-systems-all-50-states-second-edition

244 Institute on Taxation and Economic Policy, "ITEP Microsimulation Tax Model — Frequently Asked Questions," 2021, https://itep.org/modelfaq/

245 Raymond J. Ring, Jr., "Consumers' Share and Producers' Share of the General Sales Tax," National Tax Journal, March 1999, https://www.jstor.org/stable/41789377?seq=1

246 Massachusetts Department of Revenue, "Blue Book Reports — Department of Revenue," Commonwealth of Massachusetts, last update April 16, 2021, https://www.mass.gov/lists/blue-book-reports-department-of-revenue

247 Meg Wiehe et al., "Appendix B: ITEP Tax Inequality Index and Additional Data," Institute on Taxation and Economic Policy, October 2018, https://itep.sfo2.digitaloceanspaces.com/whopays-ITEP-2018_appendixB.pdf

248 Jared Walczak, "'Who Pays?' Doesn't Tell Us Much About Who Actually Pays State Taxes," Tax Foundation, October 18, 2018, https://taxfoundation.org/itep-who-pays-analysis/

249 Meg Wiehe et al., "Who Pays? A Distributional Analysis of the Tax Systems in All 50 States," Institute on Taxation and Economic Policy, October 2018, https://itep.sfo2.digitaloceanspaces.com/whopays-ITEP-2018.pdf

250 Ibid.

251 Olivia Giovetti, "How does education affect poverty? It can help end it," Concern Worldwide U.S., August 27, 2020, https://www.concernusa.org/story/how-education-affects-poverty

252 Avantika Chilkoti & Denise-Marie Ordway, "How Medicaid and Medicare influence income inequality," The Journalist's Resource, March 16, 2017, https://journalistsresource.org/economics/medicaid-medicare-income-inequality-insurance-poor/

National Association of State Budget Officers, "2020 State Expenditure Report," 2020, https://higherlogicdownload.s3.amazonaws.com/NASBO/9d2d2db1-c943-4f1b-b750-0fca152d64c2/UploadedImages/SER%20Archive/2020_State_Expenditure_Report_S.pdf

253 United States Congressional Budget Office, "The Distribution of Household Income, 2016," July 9, 2019, https://www.cbo.gov/publication/55413

254 Massachusetts Department of Revenue, "Tax Year 2017: Statistics of Income Tax Returns by Quintile (1)," Commonwealth of Massachusetts, https://www.mass.gov/doc/tax-year-2017-statistics-of-income-tax-returns-by-quintile-1/download

Massachusetts Taxpayers Foundation, email message to authors, June 27, 2017

255 Massachusetts Department of Revenue, "Tax Year 2017: Statistics of Income Tax Returns by Quintile (1)," Commonwealth of Massachusetts, https://www.mass.gov/doc/tax-year-2017-statistics-of-income-tax-returns-by-quintile-1/download

256 Ibid.

257 Jared Walczak, "'Who Pays?' Doesn't Tell Us Much About Who Actually Pays State Taxes," Tax Foundation, October 18, 2018, https://taxfoundation.org/itep-who-pays-analysis/

258 Kim Reuben & Megan Randall, "Revenue Volatility: How States Manage Uncertainty," Tax Policy Center, November 2017, https://www.taxpolicycenter.org/sites/default/files/publication/149171/revenue-volatility_1.pdf

259 Jared Walczak, "'Who Pays?' Doesn't Tell Us Much About Who Actually Pays State Taxes," Tax Foundation, October 18, 2018, https://taxfoundation.org/itep-who-pays-analysis/

260 Carl Davis et al., "Who Pays? A Distributional Analysis of the Tax Systems in All 50 States," Institute on Taxation and Economic Policy, January 2015, Institute on Taxation and Economic Policy, https://itep.sfo2.digitaloceanspaces.com/whopaysreport.pdf

261 United States Internal Revenue Service, "SOI Tax Stats - Historic Table 2," United States Department of the Treasury, last updated September 15, 2020, https://www.irs.gov/statistics/soi-tax-stats-historic-table-2

   Massachusetts Department of Revenue, "Tax Year 2017: Statistics of Income Tax Returns by Quintile (1)," Commonwealth of Massachusetts, https://www.mass.gov/doc/tax-year-2017-statistics-of-income-tax-returns-by-quintile-1/download

262 United States Internal Revenue Service, "SOI Tax Stats — Historic Table 2," United States Department of the Treasury, last updated September 15, 2020, https://www.irs.gov/statistics/soi-tax-stats-historic-table-2

   Massachusetts Department of Revenue, "Tax Year 2017: Statistics of Income Tax Returns by Quintile (1)," Commonwealth of Massachusetts, https://www.mass.gov/doc/tax-year-2017-statistics-of-income-tax-returns-by-quintile-1/download

263 Massachusetts Department of Revenue, "Tax Year 2017: Statistics of Income Tax Returns by Quintile (1)," Commonwealth of Massachusetts, https://www.mass.gov/doc/tax-year-2017-statistics-of-income-tax-returns-by-quintile-1/download

264 United States Internal Revenue Service, "SOI Tax Stats — Historic Table 2," United States Department of the Treasury, last updated September 15, 2020, https://www.irs.gov/statistics/soi-tax-stats-historic-table-2

   Massachusetts Department of Revenue, "Tax Year 2017: Statistics of Income Tax Returns by Quintile (1)," Commonwealth of Massachusetts, https://www.mass.gov/doc/tax-year-2017-statistics-of-income-tax-returns-by-quintile-1/download

265 Jason Pramas, "Capitalist Veto: Popular "millionaires' tax" referendum question blocked by a pro-business SJC," JasonPramas.work, June 19, 2018, https://jasonpramas.work/2018/06/19/capitalist-veto/

266 Kurt Wise & Noah Berger, "The Evidence on Millionaire Migration and Taxes," Massachusetts Budget and Policy Center, last updated January 18, 2018, https://archive.massbudget.org/report_window.php?loc=The-Evidence-on-Millionaire-Migration-and-Taxes.html

Phineas Baxandall, "What Has Happened in Other States with High Tax Rates on Million-Dollar Incomes?" Massachusetts Budget and Policy Center, April 12, 2018, https://www.massbudget.org/reports/pdf/Other%20States%20Tax%20 Experiences%20FINAL.pdf

267 Cristobal Young et al., "Millionaire Migration and Taxation of the Elite: Evidence from Administrative Data," American Sociological Review, June 2016, https://web. stanford.edu/~cy10/public/Jun16ASRFeature.pdf

268 Board of Governors of the Federal Reserve System, "Survey of Consumer Finances (SCF)," United States Federal Reserve Bank, last updated November 17, 2020, https://www.federalreserve.gov/econres/scfindex.htm

269 Note: the number of millionaires from Cristobal Young's work is based on adjusted gross income, while the Federal Reserve Board figures obtained by Pioneer Institute use "total income," which includes "wages, self-employment and business income, taxable and tax-exempt interest, dividends, realized capital gains, food stamps and other support programs provided by the government, pension income and withdrawals from retirement accounts, Social Security income, alimony and other support payments, and miscellaneous sources of income."

Survey Documentation and Analysis, "SCF Combined Extract Data," University of California Berkeley, https://sda.berkeley.edu/sdaweb/docs/scfcomb2019/DOC/ hcbk0007.htm#INCOME

Barry W. Johnson & Kevin Moore, "Differences in Income Estimates Derived from Survey and Tax Data," American Statistical Association, 2008, http://www.asasrms. org/Proceedings/y2008/Files/301078.pdf

270 Board of Governors of the Federal Reserve System, "Survey of Consumer Finances (SCF)," United States Federal Reserve Bank, last updated November 17, 2020, https://www.federalreserve.gov/econres/scfindex.htm

271 Board of Governors of the Federal Reserve System, "Survey of Consumer Finances (SCF)," United States Federal Reserve Bank, last updated November 17, 2020, https://www.federalreserve.gov/econres/scfindex.htm

272 Ibid.

273 Board of Governors of the Federal Reserve System, "Survey of Consumer Finances (SCF)," United States Federal Reserve Bank, last updated November 17, 2020, https://www.federalreserve.gov/econres/scfindex.htm

274 Barry W. Johnson & Kevin Moore, "Differences in Income Estimates Derived from Survey and Tax Data," American Statistical Association, 2008, http://www.asasrms. org/Proceedings/y2008/Files/301078.pdf

275 Board of Governors of the Federal Reserve System, "Survey of Consumer Finances (SCF)," United States Federal Reserve Bank, last updated November 17, 2020, https://www.federalreserve.gov/econres/scfindex.htm

276 Board of Governors of the Federal Reserve System, "Survey of Consumer Finances (SCF)," United States Federal Reserve Bank, last updated November 17, 2020, https://www.federalreserve.gov/econres/scfindex.htm

277 Cristobal Young et al., "Millionaire Migration and Taxation of the Elite: Evidence from Administrative Data," American Sociological Review, June 2016, https://web.stanford.edu/~cy10/public/Jun16ASRFeature.pdf

278 Data Made Useful, "MA In and Out Migration 1993–2018," IRS Tax Data Discovery, 2020, https://irsdatadiscovery.com/ma-in-and-out-migration-1993-2018

279 Ibid.

280 Throughout this paper, we refer to data the IRS characterizes as belonging to a range of years as belonging to the latest year in the range (i.e., 2011–2012 data are called 2012 data, etc.). This entails that our figures are reflective of when the IRS received the tax returns, although these returns may represent income earned in prior years.

281 Data Made Useful, "MA In and Out Migration 1993–2018," IRS Tax Data Discovery, 2020, https://irsdatadiscovery.com/ma-in-and-out-migration-1993-2018

282 Ibid.

283 Data Made Useful, "MA In and Out Migration 1993–2018," IRS Tax Data Discovery, 2020, https://irsdatadiscovery.com/ma-in-and-out-migration-1993-2018

284 Michael Walker, "FL IRS State to State Migration," Data Made Useful, 2020, https://public.tableau.com/profile/michael.walker#!/vizhome/FL_IRS_StatetoState_Migration/YearlyAGIFlow

285 Data Made Useful, "Gross Taxpayer Migration — All States," IRS Tax Data Discovery, 2020, https://irsdatadiscovery.com/gross-taxpayer-migration-all-states

286 Cristobal Young et al., "Millionaire Migration and Taxation of the Elite: Evidence from Administrative Data," American Sociological Review, June 2016, https://web.stanford.edu/~cy10/public/Jun16ASRFeature.pdf

287 Data Made Useful, "MA In and Out Migration 1993–2018," IRS Tax Data Discovery, 2020, https://irsdatadiscovery.com/ma-in-and-out-migration-1993-2018

288 Data Made Useful, "Gross Taxpayer Migration — All States," IRS Tax Data Discovery, 2020, https://irsdatadiscovery.com/gross-taxpayer-migration-all-states

289 Jon Bajika & Joel Slemrod, "Do The Rich Flee From High State Taxes? Evidence From Federal Estate Tax Returns," National Bureau of Economic Research, July 2004, https://www.nber.org/system/files/working_papers/w10645/w10645.pdf

290 Enrico Moretti & Daniel Wilson, "The Effect of State Taxes on the Geographic Location of Top Earners: Evidence from Star Scientists," University of Pennsylvania, December 2015, https://eml.berkeley.edu/~moretti/taxes.pdf

The study defines "star scientists" as those with patent counts in the top 5% of the distribution.

291 Andrew Lai, Roger Cohen, & Charles Steindel, "The Effects of Marginal Tax Rates on Interstate Migration in the U.S.," New Jersey Department of the Treasury, October 2011, https://www.state.nj.us/treasury/news/2011/OCE-Migration%20Study.pdf

292 Emmanuel Saez, Joel Slemrod, & Seth Giertz, "The Elasticity of Income with Respect to Marginal Tax Rates: A Critical Review," University of Pennsylvania, August 12, 2010, https://www.law.upenn.edu/institutes/taxlaw/pastseminars/2 0101 1papers/SethGiertz.pdf

293 United States Internal Revenue Service, "SOI Tax Stats — Historic Table 2," United States Department of the Treasury, last updated September 15, 2020, https://www. irs.gov/statistics/soi-tax-stats-historic-table-2

294 Paul A. Coomes & William H. Hoyt, "Income taxes and the destination of movers to multistate MSAs," ScienceDirect, May 2008, https://www.sciencedirect.com/ science/article/abs/pii/S0094119007000897#!

295 Michael Walker, "FL IRS State to State Migration," Data Made Useful, 2020, https:// public.tableau.com/profile/michael.walker#!/vizhome/FL_IRS_StatetoState_ Migration/YearlyAGIFlow

296 Michael Walker, "FL IRS State to State Migration," Data Made Useful, 2020, https:// public.tableau.com/profile/michael.walker#!/vizhome/FL_IRS_StatetoState_ Migration/YearlyAGIFlow

297 Massachusetts Department of Revenue, "Raise Up Massachusetts Impact Memo," DocumentCloud, Commonwealth of Massachusetts, https://www.documentcloud. org/documents/2839106-Raise-Up-Mass-Impact-Memo-FINAL.html

298 See Chapter 12

299 Cristobal Young et al., "Millionaire Migration and Taxation of the Elite: Evidence from Administrative Data," American Sociological Review, June 2016, https://web. stanford.edu/~cy10/public/Jun16ASRFeature.pdf

300 Kate Lister, "Work-at-Home After Covid-19 — Our Forecast," Global Workplace Analytics, 2020, https://globalworkplaceanalytics.com/work-at-home-after-covid-19-our-forecast

301 Lydia Saad & Ben Wigert, "Remote Work Persisting and Trending Permanent," Gallup, Inc., October 31, 2021, https://news.gallup.com/poll/355907/remote-work-persisting-trending-permanent.aspx

302 Gad Levanon, "Remote Work: The Biggest Legacy of Covid-19," Forbes Magazine, November 23, 2020, https://www.forbes.com/sites/gadlevanon/2020/11/23/remote-work-the-biggest-legacy-of-covid-19/?sh=38dab4d87f59

303 Katy Murphy, "California leaders fear remote culture could fuel business departures," Politico California, December 24, 2020, https://www.politico.com/ states/california/story/2020/12/24/california-leaders-fear-remote-culture-could-fuel-business-departures-1350179

304 William H. Frey, "The 2010s saw the lowest population growth in U.S. history, new census estimates show," Brookings Institution, December 22, 2020, https://www. brookings.edu/blog/the-avenue/2020/12/22/the-2010s-saw-the-lowest-population-growth-in-u-s-history-new-census-estimates-show/

305 Baili Bigham, "5 Tech Tools That Are Changing The World of Remote Work," 15Five Blog, 2020, https://www.15five.com/blog/5-tech-tools-changing-remote-work/

306 Andrew Ross Sorkin et al., "Is Goldman Sachs Going to Florida?" The New York Times, December 7, 2020, https://www.nytimes.com/2020/12/07/business/dealbook/goldman-sachs-florida.html

307 Kate Conger, Facebook Starts Planning for Permanent Remote Workers," The New York Times, May 21, 2020, https://www.nytimes.com/2020/05/21/technology/facebook-remote-work-coronavirus.html

308 Massachusetts Competitive Partnership, "100 Business Survey — COVID-19 Remote Work," June 22, 2021, https://633a9a3b-a223-4c7d-b77d-ce154f6a2f3c.filesusr.com/ugd/5c57db_e3c9d71e9dd540e4a509eb47001aa87a.pdf

309 Alan Greenblatt, "The Economic Reality That's Splitting the Country Apart," Governing Magazine, January 29, 2020, https://www.governing.com/now/The-Economic-Reality-Thats-Splitting-the-Country-Apart.html

310 Kristen Senz, "How Much Will Remote Work Continue After the Pandemic?" Harvard Business School Working Knowledge, August 24, 2020, https://hbswk.hbs.edu/item/how-much-will-remote-work-continue-after-the-pandemic

Kate Lister, "Latest Work-at-Home/Telecommuting/Mobile Work/Remote Work Statistics," Global Workplace Analytics, 2020, https://globalworkplaceanalytics.com/telecommuting-statistics

Gertrude Chavez-Dreyfuss, "The number of permanent remote workers is set to double in 2021," World Economic Forum, October 23, 2020, https://www.weforum.org/agenda/2020/10/permanent-remote-workers-pandemic-coronavirus-covid-19-work-home/

Andrew Mikula, "Survey Suggests Demand for Telecommuting After COVID-19 Crisis," Pioneer Institute for Public Policy Research, May 26, 2020, https://pioneerinstitute.org/better_government/survey-suggests-demand-for-telecommuting-after-covid-19-crisis/

Megan Brenan, "COVID-19 and Remote Work: An Update," Gallup, Inc., October 13, 2020, https://news.gallup.com/poll/321800/covid-remote-work-update.aspx

311 Richard Florida, "What Happens When the 1% Go Remote," Bloomberg CityLab, December 16, 2020, https://www.bloomberg.com/news/articles/2020-12-16/what-happens-when-the-1-move-to-miami-and-austin

Noah Buhayar, "The Work From Home Is Here to Stay. Get Ready for Pay Cuts," Bloomberg Businessweek, last updated December 18, 2020, https://www.bloomberg.com/news/features/2020-12-17/work-from-home-tech-companies-cut-pay-of-workers-moving-out-of-big-cities

312 Lydia Saad & Jeffrey M. Jones, "Seven in 10 U.S. White-Collar Workers Still Working Remotely," Gallup, Inc., May 17, 2021, https://news.gallup.com/poll/348743/seven-u.s.-white-collar-workers-still-working-remotely.aspx

313 Katie Gallagher, "Upwork Study Finds 22% of American Workforce Will Be Remote by 2025," BusinessWire, December 15, 2020, https://www.businesswire.com/news/home/20201215005287/en/Upwork-Study-Finds-22-of-American-Workforce-Will-Be-Remote-by-2025

314 Kristen Senz, "How Much Will Remote Work Continue After the Pandemic?" Harvard Business School Working Knowledge, August 24, 2020, https://hbswk.hbs.edu/item/how-much-will-remote-work-continue-after-the-pandemic

Kate Lister, "Latest Work-at-Home/Telecommuting/Mobile Work/Remote Work Statistics," Global Workplace Analytics, 2020, https://globalworkplaceanalytics.com/telecommuting-statistics

315 Gad Levanon, "Remote Work: The Biggest Legacy of Covid-19," Forbes Magazine, November 23, 2020, https://www.forbes.com/sites/gadlevanon/2020/11/23/remote-work-the-biggest-legacy-of-covid-19/?sh=38dab4d87f59

316 EHS Today Staff, "Working at Home Could Become Permanent," EHS Today, April 22, 2020, https://www.ehstoday.com/safety/article/21129423/working-at-home-could-become-permanent

317 Kate Lister, "Latest Work-at-Home/Telecommuting/Mobile Work/Remote Work Statistics," Global Workplace Analytics, 2020, https://globalworkplaceanalytics.com/telecommuting-statistics

318 Ibid.

319 Ibid.

320 Andrew Mikula, "Survey Suggests Demand for Telecommuting After COVID-19 Crisis," Pioneer Institute for Public Policy Research, May 26, 2020, https://pioneerinstitute.org/better_government/survey-suggests-demand-for-telecommuting-after-covid-19-crisis/

321 Gertrude Chavez-Dreyfuss, "The number of permanent remote workers is set to double in 2021," World Economic Forum, October 23, 2020, https://www.weforum.org/agenda/2020/10/permanent-remote-workers-pandemic-coronavirus-covid-19-work-home/

322 Kristen Senz, "How Much Will Remote Work Continue After the Pandemic?" Harvard Business School Working Knowledge, August 24, 2020, https://hbswk.hbs.edu/item/how-much-will-remote-work-continue-after-the-pandemic

323 Jose Maria Barrero et al., "Why Working From Home Will Stick," Becker Friedman Institute, April 2021, https://bfi.uchicago.edu/wp-content/uploads/2020/12/BFI_WP_2020174.pdf

324 Kate Lister, "Latest Work-at-Home/Telecommuting/Mobile Work/Remote Work Statistics," Global Workplace Analytics, 2020, https://globalworkplaceanalytics.com/telecommuting-statistics

325 Richard Florida, "What Happens When the 1% Go Remote," Bloomberg CityLab, December 16, 2020, https://www.bloomberg.com/news/articles/2020-12-16/what-happens-when-the-1-move-to-miami-and-austin

326 Edward Glaeser, "Triumph of the City: How Our Greater Invention Makes Us Richer, Smarter, Greener, Healthier, and Happier," Penguin Press, 2011, 67.

327 Richard Florida, "What Happens When the 1% Go Remote," Bloomberg CityLab, December 16, 2020, https://www.bloomberg.com/news/articles/2020-12-16/what-happens-when-the-1-move-to-miami-and-austin

328 Federal Home Loan Mortgage Corporation, "30-Year Fixed-Rate Mortgages Since 1971," 2021, http://www.freddiemac.com/pmms/pmms30.html

329 See Chapter 12

330 Cailin Slattery & Owen Zidar, "Evaluating State and Local Business Tax Incentives," Princeton University Department of Economics, January 6, 2020, https://economics.princeton.edu/working-papers/evaluating-state-and-local-business-tax-incentives/

331 Leticia Miranda, Nicole Nguyen, & Ryan Mac, "Here Are The Most Outrageous Incentives Cities Offered Amazon In Their HQ2 Bids," BuzzFeed News, November 14, 2018, https://www.buzzfeednews.com/article/leticiamiranda/amazon-hq2-finalist-cities-incentives-airport-lounge

Aaron Mak, "Here Are the Outrageous Incentives That Losing Cities Offered Amazon for HQ2," Slate Magazine, November 14, 2018, https://slate.com/technology/2018/11/amazon-hq2-incredible-incentives-losing-cities-offered.html

Robert McCartney, "Amazon HQ2 to benefit from more than $2.4 billion in incentives from Virginia, New York and Tennessee," The Washington Post, November 13, 2018, https://www.washingtonpost.com/local/virginia-news/amazon-hq2-to-receive-more-than-28-billion-in-incentives-from-virginia-new-york-and-tennessee/2018/11/13/f3f73cf4-e757-11e8-a939-9469f1166f9d_story.html

Good Jobs First, "Of the 20 Amazon HQ2 Finalist Cities, 17 Have Now Released at Least Partial Information on Their Bids," 2021, https://www.goodjobsfirst.org/blog/20-amazon-hq2-finalist-cities-17-have-now-released-least-partial-information-their-bids

Leanna Garfield, "Cities are throwing hundreds of millions at Amazon to land HQ2 — here's how they stack up," Business Insider, April 4, 2018, https://www.businessinsider.com/amazon-hq2-cities-developers-economic-tax-incentives-2017-10

332 Brett Theodos, Aravind Boddupalli, & Megan Randall, "Footloose or Stuck in Place? Firm Mobility across Six Metropolitan Areas," Urban Institute, November 14, 2018, https://www.urban.org/research/publication/footloose-or-stuck-place-firm-mobility-across-six-metropolitan-areas/view/full_report

333 Bill Hethcock, "'Tremendous increase' in corporate relocations, expansions to Texas since pandemic hit," Austin Business Journal, last updated September 25, 2020, https://www.bizjournals.com/austin/news/2020/09/25/corporate-relocation-texas.html

334 Scott Rubin, "5 Companies That Have Moved Overseas For Lower Taxes," Benzinga, August 12, 2014, https://www.benzinga.com/news/14/08/4758999/5-companies-

that-have-moved-overseas-for-lower-taxes

Johnathan D. Rockoff & Nina Trentmann, "New Tax Law Haunts Companies That Did 'Inversion' Deals," The Wall Street Journal, February 11, 2018, https://www.wsj.com/articles/new-tax-law-haunts-companies-that-did-inversion-deals-1518350401

335 United States Public Interest Research Group, "Picking Up the Tab 2014: Average Citizens and Small Businesses Pay the Price for Offshore Tax Shelters," The Public Interest Network, April 15, 2014, https://uspirg.org/reports/usp/picking-tab-2014

336 Alan Rappeport, "Yellen calls for a global minimum corporate tax rate." The New York Times, April 5, 2021, https://www.nytimes.com/2021/04/05/business/yellen-global-minimum-corporate-tax-rate.html

337 Jon Porter, "'Historic' global minimum corporate tax rate formally endorsed by world leaders," The Verge, November 1, 2021, https://www.theverge.com/2021/11/1/22756934/g20-oecd-15-percent-global-corporate-tax-rate-havens-evasion-tech-giants

338 Jennifer Liu, "Some cities are paying people up to $16,000 to move there—this online directory will help you find them," CNBC LLC, March 16, 2021, https://www.cnbc.com/2021/03/16/makemymove-online-directory-of-cities-that-pay-you-to-move-there.html

339 Abigail Johnson Hess, "Program that pays workers $10,000 to move to Vermont and work remotely is now accepting applications," CNBC LLC, last updated January 14, 2019, https://www.cnbc.com/2019/01/10/vermont-will-pay-you-10000-to-move-there-and-work-remotely---.html

340 MakeMyMove, "Offers," TMap, Inc., 2021, https://www.makemymove.com/get-paid

341 The Ascent, "Average House Price by State in 2021," The Motley Fool, August 5, 2021, https://www.fool.com/the-ascent/research/average-house-price-state/

Zillow, Inc., "Massachusetts Home Values," 2021, https://www.zillow.com/ma/home-values/

342 Dan D'Ambrosio, "Is Vermont's $10,000 incentive program for remote workers working? It depends who you ask." The Burlington Free Press, last updated November 19, 2019, https://www.burlingtonfreepress.com/story/money/2019/11/19/vermonts-10-000-pay-move-remote-worker-program-does-work/4189358002/

343 U.S. Census Bureau, "Vintage Population Estimates for the United States and States," U.S. Department of Commerce, last updated December 22, 2020, https://www.census.gov/programs-surveys/popest/technical-documentation/research/evaluation-estimates.html

344 William H. Frey, "The 2010s saw the lowest population growth in U.S. history, new census estimates show," Brookings Institution, December 22, 2020, https://www.brookings.edu/blog/the-avenue/2020/12/22/the-2010s-saw-the-lowest-population-growth-in-u-s-history-new-census-estimates-show/

345 Realtor Magazine, "Which States Dominate Vacation-Home Rankings?" The National Association of Realtors, July 22, 2019, https://magazine.realtor/daily-news/2019/07/22/which-states-dominate-vacation-home-rankings

U.S. Centers for Disease Control and Prevention, "CDC COVID Data Tracker," U.S. Department of Health & Human Services, last updated April 1, 2021, https://covid.cdc.gov/covid-data-tracker/

346 Jeff Ostrowski, "Working remotely? Some cities, states will pay you to move in." The Philadelphia Inquirer, February 22, 2021, https://www.inquirer.com/real-estate/housing/cash-for-remote-workers-relocating-pandemic-20210222.html

347 Richard Florida & Adam Ozimek, "How Remote Work Is Reshaping America's Urban Geography," The Wall Street Journal, March 5, 2021, https://www.wsj.com/articles/how-remote-work-is-reshaping-americas-urban-geography-11614960100

348 Sergio Ocampo, "Places That Pay You To Move There in 2021," MoveBuddha, February 19, 2021, https://www.movebuddha.com/blog/get-paid-to-move/

Kathleen Joyce, "These 13 places will pay you to move there, analysis says," FOX Business, July 20, 2019, https://www.foxbusiness.com/features/these-13-places-pay-to-move-there

Shawn M. Carter, "Vermont, Alaska and 6 other places in the US that will pay you to live there," CNBC LLC, July 17, 2019, https://www.cnbc.com/2019/07/17/us-cities-and-states-that-will-pay-you-to-live-there.html

Glassdoor, "Cities & States That Will Pay You to Move There," June 17, 2019, https://www.glassdoor.com/blog/cities-states-that-will-pay-you-to-move-there/

Jeff Ostrowski, "Working remotely? Some cities, states will pay you to move in." The Philadelphia Inquirer, February 22, 2021, https://www.inquirer.com/real-estate/housing/cash-for-remote-workers-relocating-pandemic-20210222.html

Marian White, "5 U.S. Cities That Will Actually Pay You to Move There," Moving.com, June 19, 2017, https://www.moving.com/tips/5-us-cities-that-will-actually-pay-you-to-move-there/

Remote Shoals, "Remote Shoals," Shoals Chamber of Commerce & Shoals Economic Development Authority, 2019, https://remoteshoals.com/

349 Taylor Borden & Libertina Brandt, "You can get paid up to $20,000 just to move. Here are 11 cities and towns offering huge incentives to relocate there." Business Insider, March 7, 2021, https://www.businessinsider.com/us-cities-pay-people-move-incentives-2018-7

Finding Northwest Arkansas, "Talent Incentive," 2021, https://findingnwa.com/incentive/

350 Taylor Borden & Libertina Brandt, "You can get paid up to $20,000 just to move. Here are 11 cities and towns offering huge incentives to relocate there." Business Insider, March 7, 2021, https://www.businessinsider.com/us-cities-pay-people-move-incentives-2018-7

351 Sarah Berger, "These towns will help pay off your student loan debt if you move there," CNBC LLC, last updated January 12, 2018, https://www.cnbc.com/2018/01/03/us-towns-that-offer-financial-incentives-to-live-there.html

Alicia Adamczyk, "6 US cities and states that will pay you to move there," CNBC LLC, last updated August 31, 2019, https://www.cnbc.com/2019/08/31/6-us-cities-and-states-that-will-pay-you-to-move-there.html

352 Alan Greenblatt, "Tax Incentives: The Losing Gamble States and Cities Keep Making," Governing Magazine, February 26, 2020, https://www.governing.com/finance/Tax-Incentives-The-Losing-Gamble-States-and-Cities-Keep-Making.html

353 Sana Imran, "How To Get Tax Breaks, Threaten to Leave," Berkeley Business Review, July 16, 2020, https://businessreview.berkeley.edu/how-to-get-tax-breaks-threaten-to-leave/

354 Bill Hethcock, "Fortune 500 company to move headquarters from California to DFW," Austin Business Journal, November 30, 2018, https://www.bizjournals.com/dallas/news/2018/11/30/mckesson-relocates-headquarters-to-north-texas.html

355 Sana Imran, "How To Get Tax Breaks, Threaten to Leave," Berkeley Business Review, July 16, 2020, https://businessreview.berkeley.edu/how-to-get-tax-breaks-threaten-to-leave/

356 Kathleen Ronayne, "California Losing Congressional Seat for First Time," NBC Bay Area, last updated April 26, 2021, https://www.nbcbayarea.com/news/california/california-losing-congressional-seat-for-first-time/2528590/

357 See Chapter 1

358 Richard Florida, "The Pros and Cons of GE's Move to Boston," Bloomberg CityLab, January 19, 2016, https://www.bloomberg.com/news/articles/2016-01-19/ge-moves-headquarters-to-boston-leaves-suburbia-behind

359 Elisabeth Harrison, "GE Scales Back Boston HQ, Planning To Reimburse The State $87 Million," WBUR, February 14, 2019, https://www.wbur.org/bostonomix/2019/02/14/general-electric-reimburse-massachusetts-headquarters

Richard Florida, "The Pros and Cons of GE's Move to Boston," Bloomberg CityLab, January 19, 2016, https://www.bloomberg.com/news/articles/2016-01-19ge-moves-headquarters-to-boston-leaves-suburbia-behind

360 Mark Williams, "Ohio makes pitch to the coasts: Zero business taxes, low cost of living, great workers," The Columbus Dispatch, March 25, 2021, https://www.dispatch.com/story/business/2021/03/25/jobsohio-pitches-businesses-move-ohio-billboards-digital-ads/4699812001/

361 CBS San Francisco Bay Area, "Miami Mayor Makes Pitch To San Francisco Tech Workers — 'Thinking Of Moving To Miami? DM Me'," February 18, 2021, https://sanfrancisco.cbslocal.com/2021/02/18/covid-relocate-tech-workers-miami-mayor-billboard-san-francisco/

362 Middlesex County NJ Government, "Economic Development: Food Innovation in Middlesex County, NJ (Boston market)," January 19, 2021, https://www.youtube.com/watch?v=CW-rBbWSS84

Middlesex County NJ Government, "Economic Development: Autonomous Vehicles in Middlesex County, NJ (Boston market)," January 19, 2021, https://www.youtube.com/watch?v=MnDV4okkLhs

Middlesex County NJ Government, "Economic Development: Life Sciences in Middlesex County, NJ (Boston market)," January 19, 2021, https://www.youtube.com/watch?v=mBJavEKVK0Q

363 Janelle Cammenga, "State Corporate Income Tax Rates and Brackets for 2021," Tax Foundation, February 3, 2021, https://taxfoundation.org/publications/state-corporate-income-tax-rates-and-brackets/

Jared Walczak & Janelle Cammenga, "2021 State Business Tax Climate Index," Tax Foundation, October 21, 2021, https://taxfoundation.org/2021-state-business-tax-climate-index/

Milken Institute, "Hawaii, New York and Alaska Most Costly States for Business, According to Milken Institute; Electricity Costs Impact Rankings," April 8, 2019, https://milkeninstitute.org/articles/hawaii-new-york-and-alaska-most-costly-states-business-according-milken-institute

364 Massachusetts IRS Data Discovery, "MA State to State Migration," Pioneer Institute for Public Policy Research, 2021, https://massirsdatadiscovery.com/tax-payer-migration/state-to-state-migration

365 Tax Foundation, "Taxes in New Hampshire," 2021, https://taxfoundation.org/state/new-hampshire/

366 Andrew Cline, "Senate budget would make New Hampshire truly income-tax free," The Josiah Bartlett Center for Public Policy, June 2, 2021, https://jbartlett.org/2021/06/senate-budget-would-make-new-hampshire-truly-income-tax-free/

New Hampshire General Court, "Bill Text: New Hampshire House Bill 2 — 2021," Legiscan, last updated June 17, 2021, https://legiscan.com/NH/text/HB2/id/2412298

367 See Chapter 12

368 See Chapter 11

369 See Chapter 5

370 Orphe Divounguy, Bryce Hill, Suman Chattopadhyay, "How Connecticut's 'tax on the rich' ended in middle-class tax hikes, lost jobs and more poverty," Illinois Policy Institute, 2018, https://www.illinoispolicy.org/reports/how-connecticuts-tax-on-the-rich-ended-in-middle-class-tax-hikes-lost-jobs-and-more-poverty/

Katherine Loughead, "State Income Tax Rates and Brackets for 2021," Tax Foundation, February 17, 2021, https://taxfoundation.org/state-income-tax-rates-2021/

I. Harry David, "Massachusetts Implements Reduction in Personal Income Tax Rates," Tax Foundation, December 20, 2011, https://taxfoundation.org/massachusetts-implements-reduction-personal-income-tax-rates

371 Tax Foundation, "State Individual Income Tax Rates, 2000–2014," Tax Foundation, April 1, 2013, https://taxfoundation.org/state-individual-income-tax-rates/

Katherine Loughead, "State Income Tax Rates and Brackets for 2021," Tax Foundation, February 17, 2021, https://taxfoundation.org/state-income-tax-rates-2021/

372 "Enacted Budget: Statewide Summary," Commonwealth of Massachusetts, 2021, https://budget.digital.mass.gov/summary/fy20/enacted/

"All Government Areas — Summary," Commonwealth of Massachusetts, last updated October 29, 2007, https://budget.digital.mass.gov/bb/gaa/fy2008/app08/ga08/hdefault.htm?_ga=2.245655300.1628922508.1608951741-1551064997.1604960565Connecticut General Assembly, "HB-7424," State of Connecticut, 2019, https://www.cga.ct.gov/2019/FN/pdf/2019HB-07424-R01-FN.pdf

Connecticut General Assembly, "HB-7424," State of Connecticut, 2019, https://www.cga.ct.gov/2019/FN/pdf/2019HB-07424-R01-FN.pdf

Connecticut General Assembly, "Connecticut State Budget," State of Connecticut, December 2007, https://www.cga.ct.gov/ofa/Documents/year/BB/2008BB-20071200_FY%2008%20-%20FY%2009%20Connecticut%20Budget.pdf

373 Rhode Island General Assembly, "Title 44: Taxation," State of Rhode Island, http://webserver.rilin.state.ri.us/Statutes/TITLE44/44-30/44-30-2.HTM

374 Judith S. Lohman, "Taxable Income and Income Tax Rates in Five States," Connecticut General Assembly, December 12, 2002, https://www.cga.ct.gov/2002/rpt/2002-R-0985.htm

375 Ryan Forster, "Rhode Island Approves Tax Reform Package," Tax Foundation, June 9, 2010, https://taxfoundation.org/rhode-island-approves-tax-reform-package/Katherine Loughead, "State Income Tax Rates and Brackets for 2021," Tax Foundation, February 17, 2021, https://taxfoundation.org/state-income-tax-rates-2021/

376 Jared Walczak, "State Individual Income Tax Rates for 2015," Tax Foundation, April 15, 2015, https://taxfoundation.org/state-individual-income-tax-rates-and-brackets 2015/

377 Richard Locker, "Gov. Bill Haslam signs Hall income tax, repeal into law," The Tennessean, last updated May 20, 2016, https://www.tennessean.com/story/news/politics/2016/05/20/gov-bill-haslam-signs-hall-income-tax-cut-repeal-into-law/84044810/

378 Henrik Kleven et al., "Taxation and Migration: Evidence and Policy Implications," American Economic Association, Spring 2020, https://www.aeaweb.org/articles?id=10.1257%2Fjep.34.2.119

Silke Runger, "Personal taxation and individual stock ownership," The European Journal of Finance, October 28, 2020, https://www.tandfonline.com/doi/full/10.1080/1351847X.2020.1837899

Andrew Mikula, "Study Says Massachusetts Surtax Proposal Could Reduce Taxable Income in the State by Over $2 Billion," Pioneer Institute for Public Policy Research, June 17, 2021, https://pioneerinstitute.org/press_releases/economic-opportunity-pr/study-says-massachusetts-surtax-proposal-could-reduce-taxable-income-in-the-state-by-over-2-billion/

379 United States Internal Revenue Service, "SOI Tax Stats — Historic Table 2," United States Department of the Treasury, last updated September 15, 2020, https://www.irs.gov/statistics/soi-tax-stats-historic-table-2

380 Internal Revenue Service, "2018 Schedule A (Form 1040)," United States Department of the Treasury, last updated January 2020, https://www.irs.gov/pub/irs-prior/f1040sa--2018.pdf

381 United States Internal Revenue Service, "SOI Tax Stats — Historic Table 2," United States Department of the Treasury, last updated September 15, 2020, https://www.irs.gov/statistics/soi-tax-stats-historic-table-2

382 United States Internal Revenue Service, "SOI Tax Stats — Historic Table 2," United States Department of the Treasury, last updated September 15, 2020, https://www.irs.gov/statistics/soi-tax-stats-historic-table-2

383 IRS, Individual Income Tax Returns Complete Report, Tax Years 2017 and 2018. Table 2.1. https://www.irs.gov/pub/irs-pdf/p1304.pdf. Pioneer Institute analysis

384 IRS, Individual Income Tax Returns Complete Report, Tax Years 2017 and 2018. Table 2.1. https://www.irs.gov/pub/irs-pdf/p1304.pdf. Pioneer Institute analysis

385 Joint Committee on Taxation of the U.S. Congress, Background On The Itemized Deduction For State And Local Taxes. https://www.jct.gov/CMSPages/GetFile.aspx?guid=e1a1f68c-f946-4d17-bf02-156690094d9f

386 Joint Committee on Taxation of the U.S. Congress. Analysis by Pioneer Institute.

387 Andrew Osterland, "State and local tax breaks could be revived, but not without a fight," CNBC LLC, last updated January 20, 2021, https://www.cnbc.com/2021/01/20/state-and-local-tax-breaks-could-be-revived-but-not-without-a-fight.html

388 Office of the Governor of New York, "SALT Letter to Biden," State of New York, April 1, 2021, https://www.governor.ny.gov/sites/default/files/atoms/files/SALT_Letter_to_Biden.pdf

389 Christopher Condon, "Summers Says New York's Millionaires Tax Risks 'Downward Spiral'," Bloomberg Wealth, April 9, 2021, https://www.bloomberg.com/news/articles/2021-04-09/summers-says-new-york-s-millionaires-tax-risks-downward-spiral

390 Trevor Craft et al., "The Economic Impact of Losing the Full Deductibility of State and Local Taxes in New York State," Rockefeller Institute of Government, May 14, 2020, https://rockinst.org/wp-content/uploads/2020/05/Impact-of-SALT_web.pdf

391 Howard Chernick, "The 2017 Federal Tax Cuts and Jobs Act: Its Impact on Massachusetts and New York," University of Massachusetts Donahue Institute, 2018, https://donahue.umass.edu/documents/MB_061818.pdf

392 Chris Edwards, "Tax Reform and Interstate Migration," Cato Institute, September 6, 2018, https://www.cato.org/tax-budget-bulletin/tax-reform-interstate-migration

393 Martin Z. Braun, "Trump's SALT Cap Fuels A Wealth Exodus From High-Tax States," Financial Advisor Magazine, January 15, 2020, https://www.fa-mag.com/news/trump-s-salt-cap-fuels-a-wealth-exodus-from-high-tax-states-53587.html

394 Ibid.

395 Laura Davison, "SALT Cap Is Hurting New York City, Adams Tells House Lawmakers", Bloomberg News, 28 July 2021. https://www.bloomberg.com/news/articles/2021-07-28/salt-cap-is-hurting-new-york-city-adams-tells-house-lawmakers

396 Andy Bollman, "Your Money: Some States Are Allowing SALT Cap Workarounds. Is Massachusetts One of Them?", The Patriot Ledger, 4 August 2021. https://www.patriotledger.com/story/business/2021/08/04/state-and-local-tax-deduction-has-generated-buzz-tax-world-salt-tax-cuts-jobs-act/5482082001/

397 Rick Newman, "The Sneaky Tax Move Democrats Are Planning", Yahoo! Finance, 17 August 2021. https://finance.yahoo.com/news/the-sneaky-tax-move-democrats-are-planning-202840517.html?guccounter=1&guce_referrer=aHR0cHM6Ly93d3cuZ29vZ2xlLmNvbS88&guce_referrer_wsig=AQAAANauieO17t8rfla3XF9uFIQI7QKbDXeFOXbsTrrfZkijGx2eiAM3tMsVy13jj5UWYRQPT9lDF8XURlKbboNG46SKVxyQjxUflJnWKYXeOi32vm8bNKCf0C7ZcpLdiBmn3W5I7NGYCTER939DtjH-NkhjfVFh5Osxldwi33AJyEE

398 Ibid.

399 Lindsey McPherson & Laura Weiss, "Democrats' 'SALT' headache hangs over budget reconciliation bill," RollCall.com, November 16, 2021, https://www.rollcall.com/2021/11/16/democrats-salt-headache-hangs-over-budget-reconciliation-bill/

400 Naomi Jagoda, "House Democrats modify SALT provision in spending bill," The Hill, November 4, 2021, https://thehill.com/policy/finance/580210-house-democrats-modify-salt-provision-in-spending-bill

401 "FY 2022 Final Budget — Chapter 63D: Taxation of Pass-Through Entities", Commonwealth of Massachusetts, 16 July 2021. https://malegislature.gov/budget/finalbudget

402 Nutter McClennan & Fish, LLP, "Overriding the Governor, Massachusetts Legislature Gives Pass-Through Entity Owners a Workaround to Federal SALT Deduction Cap," JD Supra, LLC, October 26, 2021, https://www.jdsupra.com/legalnews/overriding-the-governor-massachusetts-4151301/

403 This statistic was derived from the following source: Internal Revenue Service, "Individual Income and Tax Data, by State and Size of Adjusted Gross Income, Tax Year 2018 (Massachusetts)". https://www.irs.gov/statistics/soi-tax-stats-historic-table-2. First considered was the AGI for individuals making over $1 million a year in Massachusetts which amounted to $70,693,909. Second, income from Partnership/S corporations net income (less loss) was reported as $13,789,577. Third, net capital gain (less loss) was reported as $24,416,803. According to IRS break down of capital gains for tax year 2018 — see: "Returns with Income or Loss

from Sales of Capital Assets Reported on Form 1040, Schedule D: Selected Items, by Size of Adjusted Gross Income, Tax Year 2018 (Filing Year 2019) https://www. irs.gov/pub/irs-soi/18in14acg.xls" — 40.5% of the net capital gain (less loss) for taxpayers with incomes over $1 million came from Partnerships/S corporations, amounting to $9,888,805. Thus, 33% of AGI for taxpayers with incomes over $1 million is attributable to Partnerships/S corporations.

404 The Commonwealth of Massachusetts, "House Docket 4019", 19 February 2021. Italics added by author. https://malegislature.gov/Bills/192/H86.Html

405 Katherine Loughead, "State Individual Income Tax Rates and Brackets for 2021," Tax Foundation, February 17, 2021, https://taxfoundation.org/state-income-tax-rates-2021/

406 Kazim P. Ozyurt, "Raise Up Statistics (9-24-2015)," Massachusetts Department of Revenue, September 24, 2015, Raise Up Statistics (9-24-2015).xlsx

407 United States Internal Revenue Service, "SOI Tax Stats — Historic Table 2," United States Department of the Treasury, last updated September 15, 2020, https://www. irs.gov/statistics/soi-tax-stats-historic-table-2

Kazim P. Ozyurt, "Raise Up Statistics (9-24-2015)," Massachusetts Department of Revenue, September 24, 2015, Raise Up Statistics (9-24-2015).xlsx

408 Kazim P. Ozyurt, "Raise Up Statistics (9-24-2015)," Massachusetts Department of Revenue, September 24, 2015, Raise Up Statistics (9-24-2015).xlsx

409 Ibid.

410 Smith & Howard, "2018 Tax Cuts & Jobs Act Overview," March 2018, https://www. smith-howard.com/2018-tax-cuts-jobs-act-overview/

411 United States Internal Revenue Service, "SOI Tax Stats — Historic Table 2," United States Department of the Treasury, last updated September 15, 2020, https://www. irs.gov/statistics/soi-tax-stats-historic-table-2

412 Katherine Loughead, "State Individual Income Tax Rates and Brackets for 2021," Tax Foundation, February 17, 2021, https://taxfoundation.org/state-income-tax-rates-2021/

413 Tax Policy Center, "State Treatment of Itemized Deductions," Urban Institute & Brookings Institution, December 8, 2020, https://www.taxpolicycenter.org/ statistics/state-treatment-itemized-deductions

Franchise Tax Board, "Tax deduction — Charitable contributions and others," State of California, last updated July 15, 2020, https://www.ftb.ca.gov/about-ftb/ newsroom/tax-news/march-2019/tax-deduction.html

414 Oregon Department of Revenue, "Oregon 2020 Individual Income Tax Guide," State of Oregon, last updated March 26, 2021, https://www.oregon.gov/dor/forms/ FormsPubs/publication-or-17_101-431_2020.pdf

415 Board of Governors of the Federal Reserve System, "Survey of Consumer Finances (SCF)," United States Federal Reserve Bank, last updated November 17, 2020, https://www.federalreserve.gov/econres/scfindex.htm

ENDNOTES

416 Ibid.

417 Andrew Cline, "Senate budget would make New Hampshire truly income-tax free," The Josiah Bartlett Center for Public Policy, June 2, 2021, https://jbartlett.org/2021/06/senate-budget-would-make-new-hampshire-truly-income-tax-free/

New Hampshire General Court, "Bill Text: New Hampshire House Bill 2 — 2021," Legiscan, last updated June 17, 2021, https://legiscan.com/NH/text/HB2/id/2412298

201